401(k)
ESSENTIALS
For The HR Professional

Plan Administration Simplified For The 401(k) Plan Sponsor

2016 Edition

Barbara Klein, QPA, QKA

Copyright © 2016 by Barbara Klein

All rights reserved. No part of this book shall be reproduced or transmitted in any form or by any means, electronic or mechanical, including photocopying, recording, or by any information retrieval system without written permission of the publisher or author.

ISBN-13: 978-0-9968130-0-6

Second Edition
10 9 8 7 6 5 4 3 2 1

To order this book in quantity for your organization please contact:

info@401kEssentials.com

Published by 401k Essentials
209 West Anapamu Street
Santa Barbara, CA 93101-3604

www.401kEssentials.com/category/books

Printed in United States of America

This book is written to assist 401(k) plan sponsors in understanding their role as it applies to their 401(k) plan. It provides information explaining their duties, responsibilities, and tasks associated with offering a 401(k) plan to their employees. Often, the owner or officers of the company direct the Human Resources department, the Payroll department, or the Accounting department to oversee the plan. This book is dedicated to those tasked with the assignment of handling the plan.

Many business owners will benefit from this book. It explains the basic operational aspects of a 401(k) plan. Understanding plan operation is vital in fulfilling their fiduciary duties and continued qualification of the plan.

TABLE OF CONTENTS

Disclaimer	vi
Acknowledgements	vii
Introduction	ix
Chapter 1: 401(k) Defined	3
Chapter 2: Plan Document Basics	9
Chapter 3: The 401(k) Team	15
Chapter 4: Don't Miss The Deadlines	21
Chapter 5: Employee Categories	29
Chapter 6: Employee Communications	35
Chapter 7: Easy Enrollment	47
Chapter 8: Trouble Free Loans	55
Chapter 9: Vesting: Take It or Leave It	61
Chapter 10: Distribution Essentials	69
Chapter 11: Determinations and Calculations	79
Chapter 12: Testing Matters	85
Chapter 13: Plan Data Explained	93
Chapter 14: Record Retention Counts	101
Chapter 15: Mistakes Happen	109
Appendix A: Steps in Establishing a 401(k) Plan	117
Appendix B: Setting Up the Plan Sponsor's 401(k) Files	119
Appendix C: IRS 401(k) Resource Guide	121
Appendix D: IRS 401(k) Plan Checklist	123
Appendix E: IRS 401(k) Fix It Guide	125
Appendix F: FAQs on EFAST2 Filing Credentials	129
Appendix G: EFAST Registration Instructions	135
Appendix H: Key Administrative Dates	137
Appendix I: Non-Calendar Year Plans	139
Appendix J: Glossary of 401(k) Terms	141
Appendix K: 401(k) and Pension Acronyms	147
Appendix L: Illustration of the 401(k) Team	151
Appendix M: The Saver's Tax Credit	153
About the Author	155
What People Are Saying	156
About 401kEssentials.com	159
Shop the Bookstore	166

DISCLAIMER

This book provides general information on the topic of 401(k) plans. It is designed to provide accurate information in regard to a complex subject, but the author is not rendering legal, accounting, or other professional services. If legal or other expert assistance is required, the services of a competent professional should be sought. The author disclaims any implied or actual warranties as to the accuracy of the written materials and any liability with respect to such materials.

Every effort has been made to make this book as complete and as accurate as possible. However, this text should be used only as a general guide and not as the only source of 401(k) plan information. Furthermore, this book contains information that is current only up to the printing date.

It is not the purpose of this book to reprint all the information that is otherwise available to you. You are urged to read available material and learn as much as possible about 401(k) plans.

If you are dissatisfied with the limitations of this book as described above, you may return this book to the publisher for a full refund.

ACKNOWLEDGEMENTS

This book had been brewing for many years. I perceived there was no type of educational material available to 401(k) Plan Sponsors assisting them in their role of operating a 401(k) plan. During my 40 years experience in the retirement industry, I had never seen a tool that could be given to the person tasked with handling the 401(k) plan at the employer's office. I decided to create one. We are now in our second edition.

To my parents, my husband, our children, my brothers and all my in-laws - you provide me with inspiration, technical assistance, laughs, and fun.

Special thanks to Pat McFarland. She edited, created, encouraged and helped in all aspects of this book venture. We will always remember the Carnival Inspiration!

Thank you to my ABA staff. Without you, I couldn't dream these ideas. To all the ABA staff (past and present), my friends from the former "Pentabs/Corbel", RL Abedon Co., and the New Bedford Social Security Administration office, you taught me so much on this pension journey.

Finally, let me thank all my clients, professional peers, business associates, and mentors (past, present, and future). I truly enjoy this life and my journey. It seems I was destined to provide pension services in many forms.

INTRODUCTION TO 401(k) ESSENTIALS

This book is written for the 401(k) Plan Sponsor and their staff member or department assigned the role of handling the plan at the plan sponsor's office. We understand you hire professionals to administer your 401(k) plan, however, there are still tasks that are required of the Plan Sponsor.

Does your company sponsor a 401(k) plan? If the answer is yes, congratulations on offering what might be considered one of the most important benefits your employees participate in.

Did you know that the company that sponsors a 401(k) plan takes on additional roles which are created by offering a 401(k) plan to their employees? Here are just a few titles they may have assumed:

- Plan Sponsor
- Plan Trustee
- Plan Administrator
- Fiduciary
- Plan Representative

This book is designed to give you a better understanding of the administration of your plan. Every 401(k) plan is different, and this book is a guide. It will assist you in becoming familiar with terminology, operations, deadlines, processes, forms, and much more. Or, it will confirm the knowledge you have. It will not address all 401(k) plan complexities such as plan investing, fiduciary standards, and other specialty areas.

This book is to be used as a tool and reference book. Please make notes as you go. The exercise at the end of each chapter will assist you in knowing your plan better and allow you to have a clearer understanding of the tasks you encounter throughout the life of your 401(k) plan.

Just because you have hired a third party administrator (TPA), a recordkeeper, a payroll company or another entity to administer the plan, does not mean there is nothing you need to do in regard to operating the 401(k) plan. They provide services to handle the complexities, the reporting, the compliance, the plan document, and so forth. They will require you to provide information that only you will have.

The information in this book is presented for plans that operate on a calendar year basis. If your plan's anniversary date is other than December 31, certain deadlines may need to be adjusted.

Your employees, management and service providers will continue to come to you with questions. This book will help you have answers and resources to assist them.

401(k) ESSENTIALS

For The HR Professional

Chapter 1
401(k) DEFINED

Merriam-Webster.com's definition is:

401(k), noun:
A method by which the workers in a company can save money for their retirement by having an amount of money saved from their paychecks over a long period of time.

What Is A 401(k) Plan?

The answer might surprise you. It's complicated, but we will keep it simple.

A 401(k) plan is an employer sponsored retirement savings plan where both the employer and the employee contribute to the plan. The term "401(k)" is the actual Internal Revenue Code (IRC) section of the law that permits an employee to contribute pre-tax dollars into a qualified retirement plan. It was enacted in 1978.

The basic premise is that:

1. A 401(k) plan is a qualified retirement plan which secures favorable tax treatment under the Internal Revenue Code.

2. A 401(k) plan is a defined contribution plan. A defined contribution plan is a type of retirement plan that allows for a contribution (money) to go into a plan rather than the promise of a benefit coming out of the plan. There are a number of different types of defined contribution plans. These plans all establish an "account" for the plan's participants.

3. A 401(k) plan is a profit sharing plan. A profit sharing plan is a type of defined contribution plan. A profit sharing plan, established by the employer, may allow the employer discretion to contribute money to the plan on behalf of its eligible employees.

4. A 401(k) plan is also called a cash or deferred arrangement (CODA). A CODA allows each employee to choose to defer a portion of his/her pay into the plan or not (out of their wages).

401(k) plans are extremely popular with employees because they offer a convenient way of saving for retirement on a tax deferred basis through a payroll deduction. The employee "elects" in writing to have an amount taken from his/her pay before Federal and most state withholding taxes are assessed or taken. These deferred wages are subject to FICA taxes, FUTA, and other state taxes.

The investment earnings on these deferrals are also tax deferred.

401(k) deferrals are different from Section 125 deferrals which are exempt from all taxes.

To summarize, 401(k) is a feature (option) available in a profit sharing plan that allows an employee to contribute (defer) a portion of his wages into the profit sharing plan's trust account on a pre-tax basis.

What Type Of Contributions Does Your 401(k) Plan Allow For?

There are 3 types of contributions that a plan may receive:

1. Employer contributions

2. Employee contributions

3. Rollover contributions

These type of contributions have different attributes. They may be "tax deferred" or "after-tax" contributions.

Tax deferred (pre-tax) means the funds in the 401(k) plan have not yet been taxed to the plan participant. After-tax (post-tax) means the participant has already paid tax on these funds, and therefore has a tax basis on them.

What does this really mean? When the money is paid out of the plan to participants, they will be required to pay tax on the pre-tax dollars. Do not confuse this with an employee rolling over the funds into an Individual Retirement Account (IRA).

EMPLOYER CONTRIBUTIONS - made by the employer to a plan and are generally tax deductible to the employer. These funds come from the company's profits. They may be defined in your plan's document as fixed (required) or they may be defined as discretionary (optional).

- Profit Sharing, also known as non-elective (optional)
- Match (optional or required)
- Safe Harbor (required)

EMPLOYEE CONTRIBUTIONS - made by the employee to a plan from their pay (wages) directly.

- 401(k) (tax deferred)
- Roth 401(k) (after-tax)

ROLLOVER CONTRIBUTIONS - a transfer of funds into the plan from the employee's retirement funds held in another qualified plan or from their IRA. These funds could be pre-tax or after-tax.

What Are Roth Deferrals?

A 401(k) plan may offer a Roth 401(k) deferral which is also known as a "designated Roth contribution". Roth deferrals have been available as a plan feature since 2006.

Roth 401(k) deferrals are not exempt from current taxes. That is why they are deemed after-tax employee contributions. The investment earnings are allowed to grow and are never taxed. This is considered another advantage of a Roth contribution. When the funds are distributed from the plan to the participant, they will not be taxed.

Roth 401(k) deferrals deposited into the plan are treated as if they are 401(k) deferrals for purposes of limits and testing.

Are There Other Advantages Of Making 401(k) Deferrals?

Making 401(k) deferrals gives employees choices. They will choose how much to defer. They will select which investment funds they will invest their deferrals into. They will be able to change deferral amounts periodically. They may stop deferring at any time.

401(k) funds are portable. This means the employee can transfer their 401(k) account to a new employer's plan or an IRA when they meet certain criteria established by the plan in which they participate.

What Is A Matching Contribution?

Some 401(k) plans offer an employer matching contribution. In simple terms, if an employee elects to make 401(k) deferrals, then the employer will "match" these dollars by making an additional deposit. The match is deposited by the employer from the employer's funds into the participant's 401(k) plan account.

Generally, the employee will choose how these matching funds are invested. The match will be subject to a vesting schedule. See *Chapter 9, Vesting: Take It Or Leave It.*

An employer match is calculated based on a formula. Popular formulas are:

- 100% of 401(k) deferrals up to 3% of compensation
- 50% of deferrals on the first 6% deferred

Your plan could set a cap on the match. For example, 25% of 401(k) deferrals not to exceed $1,000. Your plan document will provide the parameters for your match. Your document may specify the actual formula. Or, the document may define the match as a discretionary amount to be determined by the employer annually basis. If the plan document provides for a discretionary match, there may be times when no match is provided.

Communicate the match to your employees. This will encourage plan participation.

Are There Limits On How Much An Employee Can Contribute To Their 401(k) Account?

Yes. Each year the IRS publishes the next year's maximum 401(k) deferral amount. This is also known as the 402(g) maximum. The limit is a maximum amount an individual can defer. This means no one can exceed their limit, no matter how many 401(k) plans they contribute to in a calendar year. The 402(g) limit for 2016 is $18,000 per individual.

If an employee is at least age 50, they are allowed to increase their 401(k) deferral above this annual limit. This increase is called a catch- up contribution and is limited as well. The maximum catch-up for 2016 is $6,000.

What Makes A 401(k) Plan A "Qualified" Retirement Plan?

The "special tax treatment" a 401(k) plan receives under IRC Section 401(a) is what makes the plan qualified. Some of these special tax treatments are:
- ➢ Pre-tax contributions (not currently taxed)
- ➢ Tax-deferred growth (investment earnings)
- ➢ Creditor protection
- ➢ Roth contributions (tax-free distributions)

The employer needs to follow the regulations to ensure the tax implications are protected.

ESSENTIALS EXERCISE 1

Answer the following as they relate to your plan.

Check those that apply to your 401(k) plan.
- ☐ 401(k)
- ☐ 403(b)
- ☐ Profit Sharing
- ☐ Simple
- ☐ Defined Contribution
- ☐ Defined Benefit Qualified
- ☐ Non-Qualified
- ☐ Tax Deferred
- ☐ Post Tax

Your Plan offers:

Employer Contributions:
- ☐ Profit Sharing
- ☐ Match
- ☐ Safe Harbor

Employee Contributions:
- ☐ 401(k)
- ☐ Roth 401(k)

Rollover Contributions from:
- ☐ Qualified Plan
- ☐ IRA
- ☐ Roth IRA

Your matching contribution formula is: _____

_____

An employee who is over the age of 50 may defer (contribute) a total of $_____, which includes his 402(g) limit and catch-up contributions.

Chapter 2
PLAN DOCUMENT BASICS

A basic requirement of a 401(k) plan is that it must be established and supported by a formal written plan document that complies with the Internal Revenue Code (IRC).

When tax laws affecting 401(k) plans change, the plan document must be updated. This applies to every 401(k) plan.

Why Do You Need A Plan Document?

Simply put, the laws and the Internal Revenue Service (IRS) require it. They also require the plan document be kept current and in conformance with all applicable regulations.

When a qualified retirement plan is to be offered to employees of the business, the Internal Revenue Service requires it to be formalized. This means it must be established in writing. By placing it in writing, it becomes a legal entity and sets forth all the provisions essential for qualified plan status.

- ➢ Do you know where your plan document is located?
- ➢ Do you have an electronic copy of the 401(k) plan document?

What Is In A Plan Document?

The plan document provides guidance on your plan's design and offerings as well as guidance on the legal requirements. Basically, it sets forth how your plan will operate - rules, definitions, formulas, etc.

Highlights of what is contained in a plan document are:

- Definition of terms
- Types of contributions and distributions offered
- Plan provisions for:
    - eligibility requirements
    - vesting schedule
    - retirement age and service
    - funding and investment options
    - distribution of accounts
- IRS compliance testing requirements
- Qualified Domestic Relations Orders (QDRO)

What Other Types Of Plan Related Written Materials Must You Have?

Your files should contain the following items:

1. Summary Plan Description (SPD) and any changes made to it that are attached in the form of a Summary of Material Modifications (SMM).

2. Funding Policy and Method (Investment Policy statement).

3. Participant Loan Policy.

4. Distribution Policy.

5. Qualified Domestic Relations Order Policy.

6. Board Resolutions, Adopting Resolutions or Corporate Minutes that pertain to the plan.

7. IRS Favorable Determination Letter on the plan document.

8. Plan Amendments.

9. Form SS-4 that requested the Trust Identification Number for the plan, if applicable.

10. Plan Procedures.

11. IRS Forms used to establish the plan or to request a Favorable Determination.

12. Contracts with the service providers, investment and recordkeeping providers, TPA, etc.

13. Fee Disclosure materials.

14. Fiduciary Standards and Benchmarks.

What Forms Should You Have Available For Your Employees?

There are many reasons an employee would have to fill out a form as it relates to the 401(k) plan. Forms may be available to participants in paper and/or online in electronic formats.

The following is a list of the most requested forms:

- Enrollment Form
    - Payroll deduction
    - Waiver not to defer
    - Establishment of investment choices
- Beneficiary Designation Form
- Salary Deferral Election Form
- Participant Loan Guidelines or Policies, if allowed
- Participant Loan Request and Application Form, if allowed
- Special Tax Notice

- Hardship Withdrawal Request Form, if allowed
- In-service Withdrawal Request Form, if allowed
- Termination Distribution Election Form
- Rollover Transfer Form
- Sample QDRO
- Login instructions to the investment company website

PLAN DOCUMENT BASICS

Answer the following as they relate to your plan.

ESSENTIALS
EXERCISE 2

Your 401(k) Plan Document can be found in:

_____
(State the actual physical location of the document in its written form with actual original signatures.)

Is there an electronic copy of the Plan Document?
- ☐ Yes
- ☐ No

If yes, where is the file and what is the name of the file?

Location: _____

File Name: _____

Is the Summary Plan Description (SPD and SMM) included with the new employee orientation material?
- ☐ Yes (Good job)
- ☐ No (When is it provided?) _____

Is each newly eligible employee offered their enrollment opportunity into the plan on time?
- ☐ Yes (Good job)
- ☐ No (Fix procedures)

Is there a procedure to ensure that every eligible employee has signed an enrollment form each year?
- ☐ Yes (Good job)
- ☐ No (Fix procedures)

Those who chose not to defer must make that election in writing as well. These declination election forms are stored: _____

Chapter 3
THE 401(k) TEAM

Just like in sports, your 401(k) team consists of many players and positions. This chapter will focus on the roles the team member's play.

Illustration Of The 401(k) Team

What Is The Role Of Each Team Member?

Plans Sponsor – This is the entity that adopts the Plan. Another term used interchangeably with "Plan Sponsor" is "Employer". The employer and plan sponsor are charged with all the responsibility of making sure the plan remains compliant. They will hire, fire, appoint, and remove all others from their roles to assist in the plan operations. An employer could be an individual, corporation, business entity, group, or association of employers. Employee Organizations can also adopt a plan.

Human Resources Department - This department is usually charged with the oversight of the plan internally. They are the conduit of information flowing in and out: enrollment, form distribution and collection, facilitation of 401(k) education with the broker, liaison to the investment company, processing of participant loans, distributions, QDROs and so forth. All of this usually comes through this department. They must work closely with all the other entities listed. If you do not have a formal HR department, this role would be filled by the business owner, the office manager, the bookkeeper, the CFO or someone appointed by the employer.

Government Agencies - These agencies oversee the regulatory and reporting aspects of the plan. Each division of the government has different roles and responsibilities with the 401(k) plan's qualification. Congress passes the laws surrounding qualified plans, and the following agencies have the duty to both implement and maintain adherence to them.

1. Department of Treasury and Internal Revenue Service (IRS)

2. Department of Labor (DOL) and ERISA Filing Acceptance System (EFAST)

3. Social Security Administration (SSA)

4. Pension Benefit Guaranty Corporation (PBGC)

Payroll Department - This department plays a major role in a 401(k) plan. 401(k) deferrals begin as employee compensation (wages). The payroll department is tasked with implementing the deduction, possibly transmitting the funds to the investment company, reporting these amounts on the Form W-2, deducting participant loan payments, and so on. In the event the plan requires an audit, payroll data is always requested. You may wish to read another book in our series called, "*401(k) Essentials for the Payroll Department*".

Employees - Your active or former employees may be participants in the plan. Include in this listing - participants, beneficiaries, alternate payees, spouses, etc.

Third Party Administrator - Also known as a "TPA". The third party administrator is hired to perform the management duties of administering the 401(k) plan. Their role is to assist you in keeping the plan compliant with regulations, reporting and testing.

Broker - Investment advisors, brokers, insurance agents, financial planners, etc. may assume this role. They generally assist the employees in making proper investment and contribution choices. They may also assist the plan sponsor in selecting the investment options for the plan.

Corporate Attorney - Qualified retirement plans are legal entities. It is always wise to seek tax and legal advice from the professionals. There are many rules, regulations and deadlines to follow. Seek a legal opinion when needed.

CPA - Your accountant has a number of reasons to be familiar with your 401(k) plan. If your plan is a large plan, they will provide the required annual plan audit to accompany the Form 5500. You will provide them with the amount of contributions to be deducted on the annual tax return. They also serve as tax advisors.

Investment Company - This is where the plan assets are invested. The participants may have been given the right to direct their individual plan investments. The plan's trustees actually implement these instructions with the investment company. Sometimes the investment company may also be called the recordkeeper, as it may provide the reporting on the holdings held in the plan as well.

Other Roles Not Listed On The Chart:

Board of Directors - This group of individuals is tasked with directing management in the overall operation of the business. They may fulfill some role in implementing the plan, directing plan changes and contribution options.

Management - The plan sponsor's management team is usually involved in facilitating department meetings that will sometimes touch on the topic of company benefits and policies. Additionally, employees often feel more comfortable in a group setting when they are seeking answers to questions they may have about the company and the 401(k) plan. Keep management in the loop. They can be a resource for helping encourage 401(k) enrollment and participation.

Plan Administrator - The Plan Administrator is appointed and defined in the plan document. It is an individual or entity responsible for certain plan duties. They determine eligibility, benefits, vesting and approve or deny benefit claims and appeals. ERISA mandates they must distribute the Summary Plan Description (SPD), Summary Annual Report (SAR) and benefit statements. They engage the independent auditor for the annual plan audit and maintain the plan's records. They must determine if a Domestic Relations Order (DRO) is qualified. Do not confuse plan administrator with your TPA. The Plan Administrator is the responsible legal entity. The TPA is a hired service provider assisting them (you) in their role of Plan Administrator. The TPA has no legal role in the plan.

Plan Trustee - Trustees collect and hold the plan assets in trust for the participants. The trustee is responsible for managing the plan investments unless the document clearly states that the trustee is subject to direction from a named fiduciary or investment manager.

Plan Fiduciary - A fiduciary is a person who exercises any discretionary authority or control over the management of the plan or its assets, or is paid to give advice regarding plan assets. At least one fiduciary must have the authority to manage the operation, control and administration of the plan. Plan service providers are generally not fiduciaries.

Answer the following as they relate to your plan.

ESSENTIALS
EXERCISE 3

Your Plan Trustees are:

_____

_____

Your 401(k) contact person internally is:

Name: _____

How is the above information communicated to your employees?

_____

How often does the payroll and human resource departments get together to review the 401(k) plan? _____

Does your Board of Directors take an interest in the plan?
- ☐ Yes
- ☐ No

If yes, in what ways? _____

Does your management team understand your 401(k) plan?
- ☐ Yes
- ☐ No

The TPA firm your company contracts with is:

Co. Name:_____ Tel: _____

Contact:_____ Email: _____

How often does your broker facilitate enrollment meetings or education meetings with the employees? _____

Broker Name: _____

Tel:_____ Email: _____

Your Investment Company is: _____

Website: _____

Does your plan have an assigned contact at the investment company?
    ☐ Yes
    ☐ No

Contact Name: _____

Tel:_____ Email: _____

The CPA firm listed below provides the annual plan audit for the plan's Form 5500:

CPA Co: _____

Auditor Name: _____

Tel:_____ Email: _____

Chapter 4
DON'T MISS THE DEADLINES

Have you ever missed a 401(k) deadline? Do you feel unsure of when things are due that relate to the 401(k) plan?

Which IRS Deadlines Should You Be Aware Of?

There are many fixed deadlines mandated by the IRS. They may relate to the filing of forms, tax deductions, compliance testing, contribution deposits, loan payments, distributions, enrollment, fee disclosures, penalties, etc. You should be aware of all plan deadlines.

Most 401(k) plans operate on a calendar year reporting basis (plan year end). The following table will provide an overview of some of the IRS imposed deadlines in date order. This calendar is for plan years ending December 31. If your plan operates on a fiscal year, these dates will vary.

IRS 401(k) DEADLINE CALENDAR

Jan	31	Distribute Form 1099-R to all Participants who received distributions in prior calendar year File Form 945 (taxes withheld on distributions for prior calendar year)
Feb	28	File Forms 1096 and 1099-R with IRS
Mar	15	ADP/ACP testing completed Refunds to HCEs made on or before in order to avoid IRS 10% penalty Employer contributions may be due depending on type of business entity
Apr	01	Age 70 ½ Required Minimum Distribution for first year disbursed
Apr	15	Return employee contributions exceeding limits from prior calendar year
Jul	31	File Form 5500 without extension or Submit Form 5558 to apply for extension of Form 5500 for 2 ½ months
Oct	01	Earliest date to distribute next year's Safe Harbor Notice
Oct	15	Form 5500 due with extension
Dec	01	Last date to distribute Safe Harbor Notice for the following plan year
Dec	31	Annual Age 70 ½ Required Minimum Distribution must have been made for the year Final corrections of ADP/ACP test failures for prior year must be completed

Please be sure to add these dates to your office calendar. Alert other corporate departments of their internal deadlines which will assist you in making sure all plan deadlines are met. *Appendices H* and *I* have a more complete listing of plan deadlines.

What Other Types Of Plan Timelines Or Deadlines Should You Be Aware Of?

There are many timelines and deadlines that affect a qualified retirement plan. It is important to know them and not simply rely on others to remind you. Missed deadlines may incur penalties, could impact plan qualification, and could cause funds to be taxable, or even put your employer or employees at risk.

We have placed some of the major processes into four categories: Administrative, Deposits, Compliance and Reporting.

Administrative:

- Loan payments
- Stopping deferrals when a hardship withdrawal is taken
- Age 70½ Required Minimum Distributions (RMD)
- Making distributions after receiving completed election forms
- Providing plan type documents requested by participants or other plan-related party
- Providing forms
- Providing employee data to consultants for testing
- Providing Summary Plan Description (SPD) and Summary Material Modifications (SMM)
- Enrollment

Deposits:

- Deferrals
- Match
- Safe harbor contributions
- Profit sharing contributions
- Qualified Non-Elective Contributions (QNEC)
- Loan payments

Compliance:

- Form 5500 and schedules
- Form 8955-SSA
- Form 5558
- Form 5330
- Forms 5310, 5300, and 5307
- Forms 1099-R and 1096
- Form 945
- Summary Annual Report (SAR)
- Annual participant statement with vesting
- Voluntary compliance corrections
- Prohibited transaction corrections
- Non-discrimination testing corrections
- Return of excess contributions pursuant to 402(g) limits

Reporting:

- Employee census
- Annual employer data
- Change in employer (address, sale, mergers, officers, EIN, trustees)
- Change in owners or ownership percentage
- Change in investment company
- Blackout Notice (Sarbanes-Oxley)

Top 10 Deadlines

The deadlines below are not listed in any particular order.

1. **401(k) Deferral Deposits** - Regulations require 401(k) deferrals and participant loan payments to be segregated from the company's funds as soon as administratively feasible. This simply means that the funds should be immediately placed in the plan's trust on the payroll date. For some plans the DOL has provided a Safe Harbor deadline, in no case later than 7 business days after the amounts would have been payable to the participant in cash. Large plans have a stricter deadline. The government deems the "use" of these funds by the employer for the time frame after which they were withheld from the participant until the time they reach the plan's trust as a prohibited transaction. Prohibited transactions are subject to excise tax penalties. You may be subject to a more restrictive timeframe based upon your tax withholding submission requirements.

2. **Corrections Needed For ADP and ACP Testing Failures (for plans without automatic provisions)** - Generally, the ADP test must be completed and corrected within 2½ months after the end of the plan year; however, in no event later than the last day of the plan year, following the year of failure.

If you correct after the 2½ months, penalties will apply. See *Chapter 12, Testing Matters* for further explanation of ADP and ACP testing.

3. **Fee Disclosures To Participants** - Generally, participants must receive fee disclosures annually on what fees may be assessed to their account. In addition, they must receive a quarterly disclosure of actual dollars charged to their account. Most often, the recordkeeper and investment company will assist you by providing these disclosures directly to the participants.

4. **Form 5500, Form 5500-SF and Form 8955-SSA Filings** - The Form 5500 is called the Annual Return/Report of the Employee Benefit Plan. The Form 8955-SSA is called the Annual Registration Statement Identifying Separated Participants With Deferred Vested Benefits. Each of these forms is due within seven months of the end of the plan year, unless extended. The Form 8955-SSA is only required in years when there are participants to report. The Form 5500 is due every year. Form 5500-EZ is available to owner-only plans.

5. **Summary Annual Report (SAR) and Summary of Material Modifications (SMM) Distributed** - The SAR must be provided to participants and beneficiaries each year no later than the last day of the 9th month after the end of the plan year, or as extended. The SMM is created when a plan amendment changes something in the Summary Plan Description (SPD). The deadline for the SMM distribution is within 210 days after the end of the plan year of the adoption of the modifications.

6. **Plan Document Amendments and Restatements** - The IRS will provide the dates for the plan restatements based upon the legislation that requires the restatement. In general, plans must be restated every six years. Amendment adoption dates may vary dependent on what provision is being amended.

7. **Enrolling New Participants** - Newly eligible employees must be provided enrollment forms before their date of plan entry. Failure to provide and offer the opportunity to enroll is costly to the employer.

8. **Safe Harbor Notice Distribution** - The notice must be distributed to participants at least 30 days prior to the beginning of the plan year and no more than 90 days before the first day of the plan year.

9. **Summary Plan Description (SPD) Distribution** - The SPD must be provided to participants and beneficiaries of the plan within 120 days after the plan is subject to reporting. Updates are due every five years if the plan is amended, ten years if not. Make sure every newly eligible participant is provided an SPD.

10. **Required Minimum Distributions (RMD)** - The first required minimum distribution must begin by the April 1 following the attainment of age 70½. Subsequent RMDs must be paid by the end of each calendar year.

DON'T THE MISS DEADLINES

Answer the following as they relate to your plan.

ESSENTIALS
EXERCISE 4

Which internal departments need to know about your 401(k) plan's deadlines? (Examples: Finance, HR, Payroll, Legal, etc.)

_____   _____

_____   _____

How often do you schedule your 401(k) enrollment meetings with your employees, advisors and the investment company?
- ☐ Annually
- ☐ Semi annually
- ☐ Quarterly
- ☐ Other: _____

After the end of the year, when do you provide your Third Party Party Administrator (TPA) your employee census? Within:
- ☐ 2 weeks after year-end (Perfect)
- ☐ 30 days after year-end (Good)
- ☐ 60 days after year-end (Cutting it close)
- ☐ Other: _____

Does your payroll department conduct an audit on participant loan payments each year to ensure they began on time, stop when fully paid and that payments were transmitted promptly?
- ☐ Yes (Good job)
- ☐ No (Why not?): _____

Have you entered these important deadlines into your department's general calendar so you stay on top of these regulatory deadlines?
- ☐ Yes (Good job)
- ☐ No (Why not?): _____

Have you confirmed your participants are receiving fee disclosures from the investment company?
- ☐ Yes
- ☐ No

27

Chapter 5
EMPLOYEE CATEGORIES

Everyone related to your 401(k) plan may wear a variety of different hats. This goes for your employees, the business owners, the vendors, and everyone involved. With 401(k) plans you need to understand certain terminology and how an employee is deemed to be included in a particular grouping or category. Your plan document and regulations may also define these categories.

What Am I?

Employee - Anyone employed by the plan sponsor, including the owners.

- "Eligible" employees have met the plan's eligibility provisions (age and service)
- "Ineligible" employees have not met the plan's eligibility provisions

Participant - Anyone who has met the plan's eligibility provision and is not in an excluded class.

- "Active" are currently employed with the employer
- "Terminated" have terminated employment with the employer
- "Separated" have terminated employment and have begun receiving benefits
- "Beneficiary" is the designated benefit recipient of a deceased participant's account

➤ "Alternate Payee" is designated pursuant to Qualified Domestic Relations Order (QDRO) and has a right to a portion of a participant's account

➤ "Inactive" may be someone who is on a Leave of Absence (LOA) or receiving Worker's Compensation. They are still employed but have no compensation.

Highly Compensated Employee (HCE) - The Internal Revenue Code defines a Highly Compensated Employee as one who:

➤ was a 5% or greater owner at any time during the current year or the preceding year;

or

➤ had compensation from the employer in excess of $80,000 as indexed, during the preceding year, and if the employer elects, was in the top 20 percent of employees' compensation. (The $80,000 amount is adjusted annually for inflation. The amount for 2015 and 2016 is $120,000).

Non-Highly Compensated Employee (NHCE) - Anyone not deemed a Highly Compensated Employee.

Key Employee - An employee is a Key Employee only if he is:

➤ at least a 5% owner; or

➤ a 1% up to 4.99% owner who received more than $155,000 as indexed in compensation from the company in 2016*; or

➤ an officer of the company who received more than $170,000 in compensation during 2016*.

*These amounts are indexed each year.

Non-Key Employee - Anyone not designated a Key Employee.

What Role Does This Category Have In A 401(k) Plan?

Employees (including owners) are the only individuals who can participate in a 401(k) plan.

Participants are individuals who meet the plan's defined eligibility provisions and have begun plan participation on their dates of entry. The definition of eligibility is fundamental to the plan and is the basis on which one becomes a participant. This is a vital facet of the plan and is key to continuing to maintain the plan's qualified status. It is imperative that you accurately calculate one's eligibility for the plan. Be sure to provide an enrollment kit and SPD to every eligible employee.

Highly Compensated and Non-Highly Compensated Employee groups are used in non-discrimination testing within the plan, with the exception of top-heavy testing. Tests that would use these groups include:

- Actual Deferral Percentage Test (ADP)
- Actual Contribution Percentage Test (ACP)
- Minimum Participation
- Coverage Test
- Comparable Benefits

Key and Non-Key Employee groups are used in top-heavy testing only.

Are These Categories Reported To Any Entity Or Agency?

In general, participant categories are reported on the annual Form 5500. For example: the Form 5500 requires the number of participants to be reported as of the beginning and end of the plan year, including sub-categories Active and Terminated. The Form 5500 is filed with the

Department of Labor (EFAST) and shared with the IRS. Form 8955-SSA is filed with the IRS and shared with the Social Security Administration (SSA). Other IRS forms require reporting by groups.

Your TPA may bill for services based upon the number of individuals in these various groups.

If your plan is selected for audit by a government agency such as the Internal Revenue Service or Department of Labor, this government agency will confirm which group your employees are categorized in, to ensure proper reporting and testing.

EMPLOYEE CATEGORIES

Answer the following as they relate to your plan.

ESSENTIALS
EXERCISE 5

Your Key Employees are:

_____   _____

_____   _____

_____   _____

How many Highly Compensated Employees are in your ADP testing this year? _____

As reported on your last Form 5500:

1. How many "active" participants are listed? _____
2. How many "terminated" participants are listed? _____
3. How many participants have account balances? _____

Why haven't the terminated participants been paid out of the plan?
_____

Do you have any "beneficiaries" with accounts in the plan?
- ☐ Yes
- ☐ No

Do we have any "alternate payees" with accounts in the plan?
- ☐ Yes
- ☐ No

What are the entry dates available to your newly eligible participants?
- ☐ Immediate   ☐ Semi-annual
- ☐ Monthly   ☐ First day of plan year
- ☐ Quarterly   ☐ Other

Chapter 6
EMPLOYEE COMMUNICATIONS

Employees, participants, spouses, beneficiaries and alternate payees all have reason to discuss or request items regarding the 401(k) plan. Keeping the lines of communication open contribute to a successful 401(k) plan.

This chapter will review some of the tasks, forms, events and communications required from and provided to a 401(k) interested party. Contact your TPA if you have questions on the purpose, the timeline, and/or where to obtain this information.

What Must You Provide To The Employees Each Year?

The following list will get you started. Both the IRS and Department of Labor require certain disclosures be provided to plan participants and their beneficiaries. Please note, you only need to provide the "beneficiary" these items if the participant is deceased and the account deemed to be the beneficiary's remains in the plan.

- Summary Annual Report
- Annual Benefit Statement (including vesting)
- Fee Disclosures
- Enrollment Form

Are There Other Items You Must Provide To The Participants?

Certain situations require additional disclosures and notices. When in doubt, always ask your TPA or recordkeeper. To follow is a list of items that you may periodically provide or provide under certain circumstances:

- Summary Plan Description (SPD)
- Summary of Material Modifications (SMM)
- Change in Enrollment Form to modify the 401(k) deferral amount or to stop deferrals
- Loan Policy
- Loan Application
- Distribution Policy
- Distribution Election Form and Special Tax Notice
- Qualified Domestic Relations Order Policy
- Form 1099-R
- Blackout Notice
- Beneficiary Designation Form
- Notice of Plan Termination

Is There A Timeframe In Which You Must Provide These Items?

The IRS and Department of Labor have set certain deadlines. Your plan policies may also dictate timelines. Please note:

EMPLOYEE COMMUNICATIONS

- **Summary Plan Description** - It must be furnished within the later of 120 days after the plan is established, or 90 days after the employee becomes eligible for the plan, or the employee starts receiving benefits as a beneficiary. You may wish to place it in your new employee orientation packets to ensure they are received timely.

- **Summary of Material Modifications** - It must be furnished within 210 days after the close of the plan year to which the change is applicable.

- **Change in Enrollment Form** - This form is used to modify deferral amounts or to stop deferrals. It should be available to employees at all times. Be sure the payroll department has copies to hand out as well. Changes are to be made on a go-forward basis only. Your plan document should tell you how often participants can modify their deferral amounts. Employees can stop deferrals at any time.

- **Loan Policy** - Make the policy available upon request.

- **Loan Application** - Provide the application to the employee immediately upon request. The application may be available online by the investment company.

- **Distribution Election Form and Special Tax Notice** - Provide to employees immediately upon request, unless your plan has a specific timeframe in place. If the plan offers immediate distributions, consider providing these to the employee as a part of the termination process by including in the termination packet or at the exit interview. These forms may be made available online.

- **Qualified Domestic Relations Order Policy** - You should have a written policy on the process of handling a potential Qualified Domestic Relations Order (QDRO) when a participant is divorcing.

- **Form 1099-R** - Must be provided to the participant by the January 31st following the distribution of benefits or loan default that took place during the prior calendar year. Verify who will prepare and send the form to the IRS and the participant.

- **Blackout Notice** - Communicates the period of time during which participants are NOT allowed to modify their investment allocations. Loans and distributions may not be allowed during this period. The notice is to be provided to employees at least 30 days but not more than 60 days prior to certain events such as a change in a service provider or investment company.

- **Beneficiary Designation Form** - To be completed and updated by all plan participants reflecting who will be the beneficiary of their account in the event their death. Be sure participants update their forms when a life event takes place. They may wish to change their designation of who should receive the account upon their marriage, divorce, death or other event.

- **Notice of Plan Termination** - Communicates the plan is going to close down and no longer operate. It notifies all plan participants of certain information such as the proposed date of plan termination, that affected participants will become 100% vested and what the termination process might entail.

What Life Events Might Require An Interested Party To Communicate With The Plan Sponsor About The 401(k) Plan?

- Marriage, separation or divorce
- Change in name or address
- Disability
- Military deployment
- Termination of employment
- Death of the participant or beneficiary
- Heavy financial burden
- Increase or decrease in financial status

EMPLOYEE COMMUNICATIONS

A List Of Communications A 401(k) Interested Party Might Receive Or Submit:

1. Summary Plan Description (SPD)
2. Summary of Material Modification (SMM)
3. Summary Annual Report (SAR)
4. Investment Reports
5. Participant Benefit Statement
6. Enrollment Form
7. Salary Deferral Election Form
8. Safe Harbor Notice
9. Blackout Notice
10. QACA, ACA, EACA Notices (automatic features)
11. Beneficiary Form
12. Participant Loan Forms
13. Hardship Withdrawal
14. Distribution Forms - RMD, In-service, Rollover, Termination
15. Spousal Consent Forms
16. Notice to Interested Parties
17. Fee Disclosures
18. Qualified Domestic Relations Order
19. 401(k) Plan Policies
20. Special Tax Notice
21. IRS Form 1099-R
22. IRS Form W-4P
23. Plan Termination or Plan Merger Forms
24. Invitation to an education meeting
25. 401(k) promotional materials and investment materials
26. Change in fund offerings announcement

27. Instructions on how to use vendor websites
28. 401(k) plan announcements
29. Change in matching contribution
30. Announcement of profit sharing contribution
31. HCE refund due to failure of ADP or ACP test
32. Tax Saver's Credit explanation
33. 401(k) plan newsletters

This is not a complete list. It is just a sampling of items that may be required.

How Frequently Might These Items Be Required Or Requested?

Enrollment Form	Enrollment
Beneficiary Form	Enrollment and Periodic
Summary Plan Description	Enrollment and Periodic
Fee Disclosures	Annual
Participant Benefit Statement	Annual
QACA, ACA, EACA Notices *	Annual
Safe Harbor Notice *	Annual
Summary Annual Report	Annual
Investment Reports	Quarterly
Salary Deferral Election Form	Periodic
Summary of Material Modification	Periodic
401(k) Plan Policies	Event
Blackout Notice	Event
Distribution Forms	Event
IRS Form 1099-R	Event
IRS Form W-4P	Event
Notice to Interested Parties	Event
Participant Loan Forms	Event
Plan Termination or Merger Forms	Event
Qualified Domestic Relations Order	Event
Special Tax Notice	Event
Spousal Consent	Event

* Only if your plan design requires.

EMPLOYEE COMMUNICATIONS

Many of the items listed have timelines set pursuant to IRS regulations. Be sure to distribute as required to the party who is to receive the item or form. Follow instructions carefully. Penalties may apply.

Who Prepares Or Provides These Materials?

There is not a clear answer to this question. Ultimately the responsibility of providing these documents is with the Plan Sponsor (Employer). Many of the documents contain language provided or required by the IRS. Your TPA will assist you in most cases.

- If the document or form deals with plan investments, it will usually come from the investment company that holds the plan assets. Use their forms. They may not accept a generic version.

- If the document is an IRS form, there are many ways to obtain it - phone, fax, web or your TPA.

- If the document is strictly related to your plan, you most likely will find it with your plan document files or the TPA firm that assisted you with the creation and maintenance of your plan.

- If the document required is due to a company change or event, seek outside assistance to prepare the required material.

Some of these items will be requested frequently. Therefore, you may wish to keep a supply on hand or have the web link readily available so they may be downloaded easily.

Alternate Payees And Beneficiaries

CAUTION! Alternate payees and beneficiaries may need to receive the same communications as the plan participants. Once an individual is legally deemed an alternate payee by the courts, that individual must be treated the same as a plan participant as long as the plan account exists.

Upon the death of a participant, the "designated" beneficiary becomes the beneficiary. The beneficiary then assumes the same benefits, rights and features of the participant. Be sure to provide them ALL plan materials. Communication is required. The beneficiary assumes the legal requirements of a participant.

Participants Employed Versus No Longer Employed By Plan Sponsor

CAUTION! As long as former employees have accounts within the plan, you must treat them as if they are active participants. They continue to be reported on the Form 5500. They must continue receiving many of the plan materials and documents.

Continue to communicate with them. Maintain their current postal and email addresses to enable you to provide them the required information.

Understand your plan's distribution force-out rules and procedures. Force-outs relate to distributing the vested account to a former employee, beneficiary or alternate payee if the total value of the vested account is less than a certain amount. This threshold amount will be found in your plan document. If this individual's account qualifies for force-out, it may be prudent to institute the force-out so that you no longer carry the responsibility of making these communications to this individual. Your plan administrative expenses may decrease once they are no longer in the plan. See *Chapter 9, Vesting: Take It or Leave It* for more information.

Why Can't You Just Pay Out Their Accounts?

There are rules and regulations dictating when participants can be paid their account from the 401(k) plan without their consent. *Chapter 10, Distribution Essentials* will provide more details.

EMPLOYEE COMMUNICATIONS

At some point former employees with plan accounts will be reported on the Form 8955-SSA. This form communicates to the IRS and Social Security Administration that there is a benefit due these former employees from your company's 401(k) plan. Once they are reported on this form, they will not be reported on the form again until the year in which they are paid their full account balances; otherwise, SSA will advise these participants of the possible existence of plan accounts when they apply for their future social security benefits

401(k) ESSENTIALS FOR THE HR PROFESSIONAL

ESSENTIALS EXERCISE 6

Answer the following as they relate to your plan.

When do you provide the employees their Summary Plan Description?

- ☐ Upon hire
- ☐ Upon entering the plan
- ☐ When requested
- ☐ Never

Do you have plan forms available online for your Participants?
- ☐ Yes
- ☐ No
- ☐ Not sure

Where do you keep a copy of last year's Summary Annual Report (SAR)?
The location is: _____

Is your Participant Loan Policy a part of your Employee Handbook?
- ☐ Yes
- ☐ No

How often do you allow your participants to change the amount of their 401(k) deferrals?

- ☐ Anytime
- ☐ Monthly
- ☐ Quarterly
- ☐ Semi-annually
- ☐ Other: _____

When do you communicate annual vesting percentages to participants?
_____

Do you maintain a list of the Alternate Payees and Beneficiaries?
- ☐ Yes
- ☐ No

EMPLOYEE COMMUNICATIONS

What information do you keep on file for any Alternate Payees or Beneficiaries with accounts currently maintained in the plan? Where is that information stored?

_____

_____

_____

Does your plan provide for force-out distributions?
- ☐ Yes
- ☐ No

Do you currently have any former employees who qualify for force-out?
- ☐ Yes
- ☐ No

If yes, what is the obstacle that is stopping you from paying them out?

_____

Do you provide your former employees who have 401(k) accounts a Summary Annual Report (SAR) each year?
- ☐ Yes
- ☐ No

If no, why not? _____

Chapter 7
EASY ENROLLMENT

Enrolling your employees into the 401(k) plan should be easy. In many cases, this benefit will become the most important investment an employee will ever make. Make the experience positive. Provide them information that is easy to understand and exciting to look at.

Who Are You Enrolling?

The answer is eligible employees.

- Determine which of your employees are eligible to participate in the plan.

- Is there an age and/or service requirement for participation?

- Once they've met the age and service requirement, what is their actual date of entry into the plan?

- Are your entry dates monthly, quarterly, semi-annual or immediate?

- In addition to the new employees, have any of your ineligible ineligible employees increased their hours so that they could could now be eligible?

- Do you have any re-hires? If so, they could be immediately eligible upon rehire.

What Is Automatic Enrollment?

Automatic enrollment allows an employer to automatically deduct elective deferrals from the employee's wages unless the employee makes an election not to contribute or to contribute a different amount. Any 401(k) plan can have this feature. If you don't currently offer it, you might want to investigate the advantages. The plan document must detail the provision's operational attributes, if offered. Later in this chapter you will find more information on how it works.

How Often Is Enrollment Required?

Your plan document will guide you as to entry dates or the frequency at which someone could change their election. We suggest you have formal meetings at least once per year. Educate and inspire your employees to want to participate and increase their 401(k) contributions. The earlier they start saving, the better chance to meet their ultimate retirement planning goals.

What Is Re-Enrollment?

Re-enrollment is simply signing up to defer again for the next plan year. In the event of an IRS audit, it is preferable to show that each employee made a new enrollment decision for the plan year.

What Can You Do To Encourage Participation In The Plan?

Matching contributions - The easiest way to encourage participation is to offer matching contributions. Most employees will sign up if you offer a match. Surveys reflect that most participants will defer up to the level that gets them 100% of the matching dollars. No one should leave free money on the table.

Educate - It is important to educate employees on 401(k) investing to fulfill certain fiduciary requirements. Keep records of the 401(k) education program you've established, documenting it for your fiduciary standards. Consider having quarterly lunch meetings. Have the financial advisors sponsor the luncheon and provide education on 401(k) investing. Make sure the investment company's website provides educational tools.

Celebrate the plan - Highlight the benefit to the employees in a positive light as often as you can. Have a 401(k) Plan Day each year. Make it a company-wide celebration. Use posters, payroll inserts, intranet messages, inspirations to encourage, educate and motivate. Everything counts towards having the employees appreciate the benefit.

Promote the Saver's Tax Credit - Encourage your employees who are middle income families or are in the lower income levels to participate in the 401(k) plan. Promote the extra IRS incentive known as the Saver's Tax Credit. If the employee qualifies for the tax credit, it may allow them to reduce their income tax bill by up to $1,000 per year. You can see a sample flyer in *Appendix M*.

Tips For Making It An Easy Process For You

Always have an updated list of who is eligible, who is age 50+ for catch-up contributions, and who might be eligible for the Saver's Tax Credit

> - Have a timeline for annual enrollment/re-enrollment process
>   - Order Enrollment Kits
>   - Select a meeting date
>   - Confirm broker and advisors are available
>   - Select a date when you will distribute the Enrollment Kits
>   - Determine the date enrollment forms must be turned in by
>   - Alert the payroll department of the incoming forms
>
> - Communications
>   - Advertise the plan - posters, payroll stuffers, emails, department meetings, intranet and so forth
>   - Be creative
>   - Provide clear instructions to employees on accessing their accounts at the recordkeeper's website SPDs
>   - Enrollment Kits
>   - Company employee newsletters

> Enrollment Process
> - Meeting and/or online enrollment?
> - Forms: Paper and/or electronic?
> - Track: Who joined? Who has not? Undecideds?
> - Have confirmation from all of them on their decision, especially those who do NOT want to participate. You have to prove they were offered the plan in the case of an IRS audit or a disgruntled employee.
> - Brokers and financial advisors should be hands-on, assisting every step in the process. Ensure they will be available to your employees as needed.
> - Deadline: Give clear instructions with a firm deadline.

Why Have Automatic Enrollment In A 401(k) Plan?

You want a high level of participation in your plan. Automatic enrollment makes it easy for you and the employee. Approximately 60% of sizable companies now use automatic enrollment and report participation rates have increased to above 85%.

What Is An Automatic Enrollment 401(k) Plan?

A basic automatic enrollment 401(k) plan states that employees will be automatically enrolled in the plan unless they elect otherwise. The plan must specify the percentage of an employee's wages that will be automatically deducted from each paycheck for contribution to the plan. The plan material will also explain that employees have the right to elect not to have 401(k) deferrals withheld or to elect a different percentage to be withheld.

An Eligible Automatic Contribution Arrangement (EACA) is similar to the basic automatic enrollment plan but has specific notice requirements. An EACA can allow automatically enrolled participants to withdraw their contributions within 30 to 90 days of the first contribution.

A Qualified Automatic Contribution Arrangement (QACA) is a type of automatic enrollment 401(k) plan that automatically "passes" certain kinds of required annual testing. The plan must include certain features, such as a fixed schedule of automatic employee contributions, employer contributions, a special vesting schedule, and specific notice requirements. If a plan is set up as a QACA with certain minimum levels of employee and employer contributions, it is exempt from the annual testing requirement that applies to a traditional 401(k) plan (the ADP test). The initial automatic employee contribution must be at least 3 percent of compensation. Contributions may have to automatically increase so that, by the fifth year, the automatic employee contribution is at least 6 percent of compensation. The automatic employee contributions cannot exceed 10 percent of compensation in any year.

Are There Any Special Requirements Of An Automatic Enrollment 401(k) Plan?

You must provide plan information to employees eligible to participate and notify them about certain benefits, rights, and features of the plan. Employees must receive an initial notice prior to the start of automatic enrollment in the plan and receive a similar notice each future year. The employee will have the option to withdraw their money within 90 days of the date that the first automatic contribution was made. A Summary Plan Description (SPD) must be provided to all participants.

You may want to provide your employees with information that discusses the advantages of your automatic enrollment 401(k) plan. The benefits to employees, such as pre-tax contributions to a 401(k) plan (or tax free distributions in the case of Roth contributions), employer contributions and compounded tax-deferred investment earnings, may help highlight the advantages of participating in the plan. The employee is permitted to change the amount of his 401(k) deferrals or choose not to contribute but must do so by specifically notifying you or the designated party.

In a QACA, the employer may make additional contributions to employees' accounts. Employers have flexibility to change the amounts of these additional contributions each year based on business conditions.

The employer must contribute at least:

1. A matching contribution of 100 percent for salary deferrals up to 1 percent of compensation and a 50 percent match for all salary deferrals above 1 percent but no more than 6 percent of compensation;

or

2. A non-elective contribution of 3 percent of compensation to all participants.

What Is A Qualified Default Investment Alternative?

A Qualified Default Investment Alternative (QDIA) is intended to encourage investment of employee assets in appropriate vehicles for long-term retirement savings. It is a default investment fund for when participants fail to make investment decisions for their participant directed contributions.

Why Provide A Qualified Default Investment Alternative In A 401(k) Plan?

Without an approved QDIA, plan fiduciaries remain (potentially) liable for losses when a participant fails to actively direct investments. ERISA section 404(c) and corresponding regulations establish protective relief from liability if the fiduciaries conform to the regulation and default funds established by the Pension Protection Act of 2006.

In addition, a QDIA is appropriate for a 401(k) plan with participant assets that lack investment direction. Plans with automatic enrollment features should have default investments. However, there are other situations that make it prudent as well, including:

- Incomplete enrollment forms

- Beneficiary or alternate payee accounts
- Qualified Domestic Relations Orders
- Removal of Investment options
- Rollovers
- Missing participants
- Disputes

What Is The Qualified Default Investment Alternative If The Employee Does Not Make An Investment Selection?

Employers must choose an investment for an employee's automatically deducted 401(k) deferral contribution. You can limit your liability for plan investment losses by choosing default investments for deferrals that meet certain criteria for transferability and safety, such as life-cycle funds or balanced funds. Your employees must be given an opportunity to change the investment choice.

The Department of Labor has approved four types of QDIAs:

1. A Life Cycle or Target Retirement Date Fund.
2. A Professionally Managed Account based on age or retirement date.
3. A Balanced Fund.
4. A Stable Value Fund.

Engage your broker and investment advisors to assist in the selection of these funds. They are the experts.

ESSENTIALS EXERCISE 7

Answer the following as they relate to your plan.

How often do you offer formal enrollment meetings?
- ☐ Once a year
- ☐ Twice a year
- ☐ Never
- ☐ Other:_____

How often do you look at your employee census and determine who is eligible for the plan?
- ☐ Per-pay-period
- ☐ Monthly
- ☐ Quarterly
- ☐ Semi-annually
- ☐ Annually
- ☐ Other:_____

Does your plan provide for Automatic Enrollment?
- ☐ Yes
- ☐ No

Do you offer Qualified Default Investment Alternatives?
- ☐ Yes
- ☐ No

Do you provide investment education to your employees?
- ☐ Yes
- ☐ No

If yes, describe how it is offered. _____

_____

Will you plan a 401(k) Plan Celebration Day this year to encourage participation?
- ☐ Yes
- ☐ No

Chapter 8

TROUBLE FREE LOANS

Participant loans can be troublesome. Something as small as forgetting to have the payroll department start the loan payments can become an ordeal. Your payroll department and participants must be educated in loan procedures to help ensure proper payment, documentation, and operation for trouble free loans.

What Are Some Problems You Might Encounter In Administering Your Employees' Participant Loans?

As with any loan, there are certain requirements and procedures that must be followed. In a 401(k) plan, the funds belong to the plan for the future benefit of the employee. The government agencies have many rules relating to how a participant loan is made, including collateral, payments, interest rate, amortization, and so forth. If these requirements are not followed, the loan could be deemed an immediate taxable distribution or even worse, the plan could be disqualified.

Participant loans are prone to error. Many things could go wrong. Remember the goal is to have trouble free loans. To help avoid some of the common mistakes, here is a list of ten ways a loan may go off track:

1. Payments began late.

2. Payments did not stop once the loan was paid in full.

3. Spousal consent was not obtained, if required.

4. The amount borrowed is more than permitted.

5. The loan policy was not followed.

6. The interest rate being charged is not reasonable.

7. A defaulted loan was not reported on a Form 1099-R.

8. Loan payments were recorded as deferrals by the investment company and not properly applied as loan payments.

9. Loan documents were not executed (signed).

10. Loan payments were deposited but were recorded to the incorrect source of funds. For example, the loan proceeds were taken from the rollover account but were repaid into the match account. Make sure to code payments to the correct sources.

It is important to audit the active loans at least annually with your payroll department.

What Can You Do To Ensure You Do Not Have Loan Problems?

The best thing to do is to understand your 401(k) plan's loan provisions.

- Understand what your Participant Loan Policy allows

- Have internal procedures in place for assisting a participant who wishes to obtain a loan

- If there is an application to be completed by the employee to begin the process of taking a loan, who must sign the application or is the entire process electronic?

- Read a loan document to become familiar with the terms and language to ensure your loan policy is incorporated correctly into the language of the participant promissory note and other attachments

- Ensure you have a procedure to get the payroll department the information they need to start the new loan payments

- Check to make sure payments stop at the end of the term

- Does the Loan Policy offer loan consolidation or limit the number of loans a participant may have outstanding?

- Ensure terminating employees understand what happens with their outstanding loan balance once they leave the company

- Have a policy to deal with a loan if an employee starts a leave of absence

- Review your Loan Policy annually to ensure it meets the needs of the employees and the company's philosophy

- If your participant loans are all processed electronically between the employee and the investment company, ensure all transactions are posted correctly and are correct

By understanding the loan rules, your plan's loan policy, and the need to work with payroll, many problems will be avoided.

Consider writing a checklist to ensure loan administration internally is foolproof.

Simple Participant Loan Rules

Here is a summary of some of the important rules and processes surrounding participant loans.

1. Maximum loan amount a participant may borrow is one-half their vested account balance or $50,000, whichever is less.

2. Loan must be repaid within a five year period or less.

3. If the loan proceeds are for the purchase of a primary residence, the term can be extended. Usually the term is ten to fifteen years in this case.

4. Loan payments are generally made as a payroll deduction in a 401(k) plan.

5. The interest rate charged on a participant loan will most likely approximate prime plus one or two points. It must be a

reasonable rate when compared to similar loans offered at a lending institution.

6. The loan interest paid by the participant on their participant loan is usually credited back to their own 401(k) account.

7. There is no credit check required on the employee.

8. The loan paperwork is simple. It usually consists of a loan application, promissory note, amortization schedule, and authorization for payroll deduction.

9. Receiving the participant loan funds is usually quick. It may take a few days or up to a couple of weeks.

10. Loans are not taxed unless they default.

11. The cost of obtaining a loan is nominal in most cases. Generally, there is a loan processing fee paid by the participant from his 401(k) plan account at the time the loan is disbursed.

12. Most 401(k) plans allow a participant to take a loan regardless of the reason. However, some plans might restrict it to hardship situations. Your 401(k) Loan Policy will provide the details.

13. Participant loan interest is not deductible.

14. Once the loan is in effect, the terms of the loan may not be changed. If your Loan Policy provides for loan consolidation, when combining an existing loan with new proceeds, you could interpret that situation as changing the terms. But it is the only situation that would allow for it.

15. There is no early payoff penalty.

16. Participant loans are only available to active participants.

17. Loans are not reported to credit reporting agencies.

18. If the employee stops working for the employer/plan sponsor, most loan documents will require immediate full repayment of the participant loan within 30 - 60 days. If it is not repaid, it is then deemed distributed to the former employee and becomes a taxable distribution of the remaining outstanding balance.

TROUBLE FREE LOANS

Answer the following as they relate to your plan.

ESSENTIALS
EXERCISE 8

Does your Loan Policy require a minimum loan amount that must be taken when the loan is created?
☐ Yes
☐ No

If yes, what is that amount? _____

How many loans can an individual participant have outstanding at one time? _____

Is there a limit as to how many times an individual participant can take a loan in a given calendar year?
☐ Yes
☐ No

If yes, how many? _____

Does your Loan Policy allow an active employee to "transfer in" an existing outstanding participant loan from an unrelated prior employer?
☐ Yes
☐ No

What is the interest rate charged to an employee for a loan? _____

Is there a loan fee charged to the participant?
☐ Yes
☐ No

If yes, is it taken from the proceeds or after the proceeds? _____

What is the loan processing fee that is assessed to the participant?

_____

59

Are your terminating employees given the option to pay off their loan upon termination of employment?
- ☐ Yes
- ☐ No

If yes, how much time do you allow them to make the payoff? _____

_____

Who instructs the investment company or other entity to issue a Form 1099-R upon a loan default?
- ☐ HR
- ☐ Payroll
- ☐ TPA
- ☐ Other: _____

Chapter 9

VESTING: TAKE IT OR LEAVE IT

When an employer contributes funds to a participant's 401(k) plan, they may not immediately be deemed available to a participant if they were to terminate employment. In order to encourage employees to remain with their employer, monies and any earnings attributable to the employer's contributions become available to the participant over a period of time called "vesting".

What Is The Definition Of Vesting?

A participant's vested account balance is that portion of the participant's account that cannot be forfeited when the participant terminates employment.

IRS has published a glossary that is located at the back of this book in *Appendix J*. Their definition is:

> "Vesting: The degree to which a participant is entitled to a portion of his or her account balance."

All plans must provide for a "minimum vesting standard". They are called vesting schedules. While the IRS requires certain minimum vesting standards, plan sponsors have flexibility to use a shorter schedule than those required under the law.

What Makes Up Participant 401(k) Accounts?

Generally, participant accounts are established by contributions received into the plan. Rollovers from other plans or IRAs may also make up participant accounts. 401(k) plan accounts are comprised of contributions which come from a variety of sources.

Here is a list of the major sources:

- **Employee Contributions**
    - 401(k) Deferrals
    - 401(k) Roth Deferrals
    - Rollovers
    - After-tax Employee Contributions

- **Employer Contributions**
    - Match
    - Non-elective (Profit Sharing)
    - Safe Harbor
    - Qualified Non-elective Contributions (QNEC)
    - Qualified Matching Contributions (QMAC)

- **Investment Gains/Losses**

Which Of These Sources Are Subject To A Vesting Schedule?

Employee contributions and rollovers are always fully vested. These dollars originated from the employee and will not be subject to forfeiture.

Employer contributions are subject to minimum vesting standards. However, there are some exceptions which require full vesting on certain types of employer contributions.

"Safe Harbor" and "Qualified" employer contributions become 100% vested at the time the deposits are made.

What Are Minimum Vesting Standards?

For Match and Non-elective contributions, the IRS requires one of the two minimum vesting schedule options be used. They are:

VESTING: TAKE IT OR LEAVE IT

> Six-year graded vesting

> Three-year cliff vesting

Six-Year Graded Vesting

A graded vesting schedule provides for incremental increases in the vesting percentage for each year of service the participant completes. The schedule works like this:

Years for Vesting Service	Vested %
1	0%
2	20%
3	40%
4	60%
5	80%
6 or more	100%

Three-Year Cliff Vesting

Cliff vesting refers to the fact that a participant goes from being zero percent vested to fully vested at a specific point in time. Under the three-year cliff schedule, an employee becomes fully vested after he has completed three years of service.

Are There Other Vesting Schedules Available For Use?

The minimum vesting standard schedules are just that - minimums. You can always offer a more favorable schedule. You have the flexibility to use a shorter schedule than those required under the law.

Here are four examples of common alternative schedules:

1. **Immediate Vesting** - The employee is fully vested as soon as they are eligible for the plan.

2. **Two-Year Cliff Vesting** - The employee is fully vested after completing two years of service.

3. **20% Per Year (Five-Year Graded) Vesting:**

Years for Vesting Service	Vested %
1	20%
2	40%
3	60%
4	80%
5 or more	100%

4. **25% Per Year (Four-Year Graded) Vesting:**

Years for Vesting Service	Vested %
1	25%
2	50%
3	75%
4 or more	100%

How Does Vesting Affect Employee Contributions?

Participant account balances originating from 401(k) deferrals and rollovers are always fully vested. Have you heard the term 100 percent vested? Fully vested and 100% vested are synonymous.

The participant's 401(k) deferrals and the investment earnings on these deferrals are always owned by the participant and subject to specific rules, penalties or taxes. They are fully vested (100% vested).

How Is Vesting Service Calculated?

To determine a participant's vested account balance, the participant's vesting service must be calculated. There are two ways to determine service credit:

- The actual hours method - actual hours worked by the employee
- The elapsed time method - time measured from the date of hire

For each year the employee earns a year of vesting service credit, they may increase their vesting percentage in accordance with the vesting schedule.

A plan may exclude some types of service for vesting purposes. Service that may be disregarded includes:

- Years of service before age 18
- Years of service before the effective date of the plan (unless the employer sponsored a predecessor plan)
- Years of service with less than the hours requirement (which cannot be more than 1,000 in any year)
- Years of service excluded under the break-in-service rules

Check your plan document to determine what method is used and if there are any service exclusions.

Can Participant Accounts Become Fully Vested Before Having Enough Service Credits?

There are certain events that will result in a participant's account becoming automatically fully vested, regardless of the participant's number of years of service.

- Attainment of normal retirement age per the plan (typically 65)

- Termination of the plan

- Partial plan termination (full vesting to only those affected)

- The plan having an eligibility requirement of greater than one year of service (up to a maximum of two years)

- If the plan allows for it, upon death

- If the plan allows for it, upon total and permanent disability

What Happens To The Non-Vested Portion Of The Account?

After the former employee receives distribution of their vested account value, the residual non-vested funds are converted to "forfeitures".

What Is A Forfeiture?

The dictionary defines forfeiture as the act of surrendering something or giving something up. In a 401(k) plan, the portion of a participant's account balance that is not vested may be deemed a forfeiture when the participant is paid his vested account from the plan.

Forfeitures are retained by the plan. They will be used as your plan document dictates. However, in no event can the forfeited amounts be returned to the plan sponsor or be used for purposes outside of the plan.

Examples for their use are:

- Reduce future employer contributions

- Pay plan expenses to service providers

- Re-allocate to the remaining participants as an additional contribution from the source from which it came

- Reinstate prior forfeited accounts for rehired employees who previously forfeited

401(k) ESSENTIALS FOR THE HR PROFESSIONAL

ESSENTIALS EXERCISE 9

Answer the following as they relate to your plan.

What contribution sources in the plan are subject to a vesting schedule?

_____   _____

_____   _____

Does the vesting schedule exclude any service an employee completes?
- ☐ Yes
- ☐ No

If yes, what type of service is excluded? _____

Your plan's vesting schedule is called: _____

The types of contributions (sources) in the plan that are automatically fully vested are:

_____   _____

_____   _____

Your plan uses the following method of calculating vesting service:
- ☐ Actual Hours Worked
- ☐ Elapsed Time

Your plan's forfeitures are used in the following manner: _____

_____

Do you have forfeiture dollars available for use?
- ☐ Yes
- ☐ No

Chapter 10
DISTRIBUTION ESSENTIALS

The plan document will describe when distributions are allowed from the 401(k) plan. A 401(k) plan is designed to be used as a vehicle for retirement savings. The IRS, along with the plan document, imposes certain restrictions on when amounts can be withdrawn from the plan.

When Can A Participant Take A Distribution Of His Account From The Plan?

Generally, withdrawals attributable to employee contributions can be made only in the following situations, provided they are permitted in your plan document. Employee contributions may have different distribution parameters than employer contributions or rollover funds.

- Attainment of age 59½
- Termination of employment (separation of service)
- Death
- Permanent and total disability
- Retirement (separation of service)
- Early retirement (separation of service)
- Hardship withdrawal
- Termination of the plan without a successor plan

There are other instances when a participant may be required to take a distribution, meaning he has no choice. For example:

1. Correcting a failed ADP test.
2. Exceeding the 401(k) annual deferral limit.
3. Having to take a Required Minimum Distribution (RMD).

Your plan document defines conditions required to facilitate distributions from employer, employee, and rollover accounts.

What Is The Definition Of Each Type Of Distribution Available From The Plan?

Below are the types of withdrawals your plan may permit:

Attainment of Age 59½ - The employee is required to have reached age 59½. It is only available in profit sharing and stock bonus plans.

Separation of Service - In order to qualify for a termination/separation of service the employee's break with the employer must be total. The ex-employee can no longer be affiliated with the former employer in any way. A termination or separation may be due to retiring, quitting, being fired, etc.

Death - Upon the death of the participant, the beneficiary would receive the deceased participant's account.

Permanent and Total Disability - Your plan will define what this means. In general terms, the employee is unable to engage in any substantial gainful activity due to a medically determinable physical or mental impairment, which can be expected to last a long, indefinite period or result in death. Some plan documents will define it as SSI, while others may require a medical opinion.

Hardship Withdrawal - If offered, a hardship withdrawal may be made only if the distribution will relieve an immediate and heavy financial burden and the distribution is necessary to satisfy that financial need. The IRS prescribes what constitutes an immediate and substantial burden. The amount distributed cannot exceed the need. Examples: foreclosure or eviction from the home, medical expenses not covered by insurance, purchase of principal residence, tuition for post secondary education or funeral expenses. The participant will not be allowed to continue his 401(k) deferrals into the plan for a six month period.

Are All Distributions Taxable?

Generally, if the amounts were not previously taxed on their way into the plan, then they are taxable on their way out of the 401(k) plan.

A participant may be able to roll over the distribution into another tax deferred account such as an IRA or another qualified plan. These rules are complex. Each participant should check with their own tax advisor or accountant prior to making a decision to take a plan distribution.

Taxes due may be:

- Federal tax
- State tax
- Penalty tax

Roth 401(k) deferrals are not taxed on their way out of a plan because they were taxed on their way into the plan.

What Is The Tax Due On A Distribution?

This is a complicated area. Encourage the employee to seek tax advice before taking a plan distribution. Never give tax advice.

When a participant chooses (elects) a lump sum distribution (cash out), the IRS requires 20% of the distribution be deducted and remitted to the IRS in the form of federal income tax. It is remitted by the plan to the IRS directly. The participant has an option to have state withholding paid at that time. Check to see if your state requires tax withholding from 401(k) plan distributions.

CAUTION! This does not mean this is the only tax due. The employee will prepare his personal tax return and the final calculation will then be made based upon his tax bracket at that time. He may owe more or less. This holds true for state tax as well. At the time he files his federal tax return, he will true-up for any tax and/or penalty tax due.

Are There Penalties When Taking A Distribution From The Plan?

Penalty taxes may apply to distributions from a 401(k) plan.

The most common penalty is known as the 10% Early Withdrawal Penalty. The IRS imposes a penalty tax (in addition to the regular ordinary income tax due) when an employee takes a taxable distribution prior to his attainment of age 59½. There are exceptions to this rule. It is important that a participant engage his tax advisor prior to taking a distribution to be sure he understands the tax implications of taking a plan distribution.

Who Is Involved In The Distribution Process?

Distributions from a 401(k) Plan require forms and consent. When money leaves a qualified retirement plan, it becomes a significant transaction. There are many procedures, rules, and regulations surrounding funds leaving a plan.

Let's break it down into groups:

1. The 401(k) Plan document will define the rules surrounding how and when a distribution may be taken from the plan. The plan's policies will describe how to go about it.

2. The Investment Company may have their own forms that need to be completed and signed by the participant and the trustee or it may be done online. The investment company will not release funds unless it is authorized by a plan representative with the authority to direct them to do so. They may provide tax reporting to the government.

3. The Employer and/or Trustee will direct the transaction, may distribute the forms to the participant, authorize the process, and communicate with all parties.

4. The Employee or former employee, also known as the plan participant, is the recipient of the distribution. They should

seek their own tax advice on the prudency of taking a distribution. They are required to consent and sign. In some cases, spousal consent may also be required. If a hardship withdrawal is requested, the employee may need to provide substantiating materials to ensure compliance of need and amount.

5. Generally, your TPA will verify forms, determine vesting, and check for accuracy based on the data provided by the employer and investment company. They will facilitate distribution, confirm the distribution is authorized, provide any missing forms required and review materials for accuracy.

6. The Government agencies (federal and state tax agencies) will receive withholding taxes and reporting forms on distributions. There are timelines to follow to avoid penalties.

What Forms Are Related Or Needed For Distributions Taken From A 401(k) Plan?

- **Employee**
  - Election Form
  - Special Tax Notice
  - Spousal Consent
  - IRS Form 1099-R (reports distribution to IRS)
  - IRS Form W-4P (for periodic distributions, how much to withhold)

- **Government**
  - IRS Form 1099-R
  - IRS Form 1096 (transmittal sheet to IRS for Form 1099-Rs)
  - IRS Form 945 (reports total federal withholding)

Can We Force Former Employees To Take Distribution Of Their Account From The Plan?

This is a complicated question. The answer is yes and no.

Required Minimum Distributions are forced pursuant to the law and the plan document. Not all participants who have attained age 70½ can be forced. Your plan document will advise you. If the participant is an owner, they will be forced to take minimums. If they are not an owner but are still employed, your plan document will state how it works. If they are not an owner but have terminated employment, they will be forced.

If you have a terminated employee who has not reached age 70½, it is dependent on your plan document.

If the terminated participant has less than a $200 vested account balance, the answer is usually yes, you can force them out and pay their vested account balance without their consent.

If the terminated participant has less than a $1,000 but more than a $200 vested account balance, the answer again is usually yes, you can force them out and pay their account without their consent. However, federal tax withholding must be taken and remitted. The tax withholding is 20% of the vested account balance.

If the terminated participant's vested account balance is between $1,000 and $5,000, you may be able to force a distribution or rollover to an IRA with a bit of work. You will have to give them the opportunity to complete a distribution election form. Your TPA should guide you through this process.

If the terminated participant has more than a $5,000 vested account balance, no, you cannot force a distribution.

What Happens When You Cannot Locate A Former Employee?

There is a term used in the industry for this situation, "Missing Participants".

Reasonable steps to locate the former employee are required due to fiduciary obligations under ERISA. There are a number of options:

- Contact the last known address on file with the investment company or your health plan's records.

- Contact the designated beneficiary. The form on which they designated their beneficiary may have an address and name. This individual probably knows how to reach them.

- Look up their emergency contact information that you had on file in their employee records or job application and contact this person.

- Use internet search tools.

- Ask some of their former department associates (employees) who may still keep in touch with them.

If they qualify to be "forced" out of the plan, you must have documented the steps you took to find them. You cannot just simply pay them out of the plan. The IRS requires you to have demonstrated and documented the efforts you took to try to communicate and provide them with their distribution election forms.

Keep good records of your attempts to locate former employees.

What Is A Residual Distribution?

Sometimes a former employee has received his distribution from the plan but a very small balance remains. The remaining amount will need to be distributed. We call this a residual distribution amount.

This small amount in the account may come from contributions or investment gains posted after the distribution was made. For instance, in a safe harbor 401(k) plan for which the employer allocates a 3% safe harbor contribution at the end of the plan year, contributions cannot be subject to a last day of employment rule. That means any participant eligible at any point during the year is entitled to the contribution even if he or she terminated employment earlier in the year.

Can You Rely On The Original Executed Distribution Election Forms For Paying Out The Residual Amount?

If the original distribution was made within 180 days, generally the plan can issue a distribution of the residual amount using the same method as the initial payment. If it has been more than 180 days, the account is subject to the distribution rules in the same manner as if there had been no previous distribution paid. In this situation, the residual balance may be below the forced distribution threshold and can be processed as such.

DISTRIBUTION ESSENTIALS

Answer the following as they relate to your plan.

ESSENTIALS EXERCISE 10

Does your plan allow hardship distributions?
- ☐ Yes
- ☐ No

Does the plan have any missing participants?
- ☐ Yes
- ☐ No

What is your protocol for attempting to contact missing participants?

_____

_____

What level can you force-out a terminated participant account, assuming you have tried to contact them?
- ☐ More than $200
- ☐ Less than $1000
- ☐ More than $1000 but less than $5000

Every time you provide former employees with Distribution Election forms, do you include the Special Tax Notice with the forms?
- ☐ Yes (Good job)
- ☐ No (Change your procedures to ensure you do)

Your plan document stipulates the Required Minimum Distributions be made to the following:
- ☐ Owners who are at least age 70½
- ☐ Non-owners who are still employed and are at least age 70½
- ☐ Former employees who are at least age 70½ (not employed)

Your plan's Form 1099-Rs are prepared by: _____

Chapter 11
DETERMINATIONS AND CALCULATIONS

401(k) plans have a number of determinations and calculations that must be completed each year. Determinations may simply be application of data, based upon certain criteria. Not all calculations are complicated math computations.

What Kinds Of Determinations Or Calculations Does A 401(k) Plan Encounter?

401(k) plans are complicated to say the least. Deadlines, regulations, compliance testing are some of the ways they have become known for their complexities.

It starts when implementing a 401(k) plan. You will need to determine the provisions of the plan. You select options available from a list of what is available under the law. Eligibility, vesting, contributions are just a few of the areas where you will make decisions.

Who is eligible for the plan? Your advisors may assist you in the design and selections for your 401(k) plan. Is figuring who is eligible a determination or a calculation? It is both. Every employee is reviewed with their own set of data. How old are they? How long have they worked for you? Did they meet the age requirement? Did they meet the service requirement? What is their date of entry into the plan? What is their normal retirement date? Are they a Key Employee this year? Are they a Highly Compensated Employee this year?

Calculations can be complex. Something that seems straightforward like how much an employee is going to receive for a profit sharing contribution might not be so simple. If the plan is contributing a 3% non-elective profit sharing contribution to each employee, what is the total amount? The answer is the eligible compensation for each employee times 3% of that amount. However, before you apply the formula, you would have needed to determine what is eligible compensation for each of the employees.

Look in the plan document and see if the definition of compensation excludes anything. Does the plan ignore compensation earned before the employee's date of plan entry? Does the plan ignore overtime? There are a lot of variables.

As you can see, determinations and calculations can be inter-related.

List Of Determinations And Calculations

The following is a list of types of determinations and calculations that are made in a 401(k) plan. This is not a complete list. Its purpose is to demonstrate the variety of formulas, calculations, applications and transactions the plan encounters. This is why you need the assistance of a competent TPA.

1. Plan eligibility:

    a. Age
    b. Service and hours worked
    c. Date of entry

2. Years of service:

    a. Hours worked
    b. Elapsed time
    c. Break-in-service

3. Vesting:

    a. Age
    b. Years of service
    c. Hours
    d. Application of the vesting schedule

4. Employee Categories:

    a. Eligible employees
        i. Active participant
        ii. Inactive participant

DETERMINATIONS AND CALCULATIONS

        iii. Terminated participant
        iv. Retiree
        v. Disabled participant
        vi. Deceased participant
        vii. Alternate payee
        viii. Beneficiary
   b. Ineligible employee
        i. Too young
        ii. Not enough service
        iii. Excluded due to a classification or plan document specific language

5. Key and Non-Key Employee.

6. Highly Compensated Employee (HCE) and Non-Highly Compensated Employee (NHCE).

7. Family attribution for ownership.

8. Controlled Groups and Affiliated Service Groups of Business.

9. Normal retirement date:

   a. Age
   b. Service
   c. Assignment of the actual date

10. Compensation:

   a. Maximum (as set forth by IRS annually)
   b. Plan compensation
   c. Excluded compensation
   d. Time frame

11. Trust accounting on plan assets:

   a. Balance Sheet
        i. Asset classifications
        ii. List of each investment held and current market value
        iii. Receivables
        iv. Liabilities
   b. Income and Expense Report
        i. Contributions by type
        ii. Rollovers and transfers

iii. Gains/losses listed by type
iv. Distributions by type
v. Expenses by type
c. Prohibited transactions

12. Contributions and Forfeitures:

    a. Deferrals
        i. Pre-tax
        ii. Roth
        iii. Catch-up
    b. Match
    c. Profit Sharing
    d. Safe Harbor
    e. Qualified Non-elective (QNEC) and Qualified Match (QMAC)
    f. After-tax
    g. Re-characterization
    h. Methods used for allocation
        i. Compensation
        ii. Age
        iii. Units
        iv. Classifications or Employee Groups
    i. Top-heavy minimum
    j. Forfeitures
    k. Deposit deadlines

13. Maximum Limits:

    a. Deferrals
    b. Employer contributions
    c. Deductions
    d. Annual additions
    e. Compensation

14. Investment Gains and Losses:

    a. Reconcile for plan totals
    b. Reconcile and allocate for each participant
    c. Allocate to sources (deferral, match, rollover, etc.)

15. Participant Loans:

    a. Maximum available
    b. Consolidation of old and new loan

DETERMINATIONS AND CALCULATIONS

    c. Amortization schedule
    d. Application of payments to schedule (principle and interest)
    e. Application of payments to sources
    f. Determination of interest rate
    g. Determination of participant's credit worthiness

16. Distributions:

    a. Vesting
    b. Forfeitures
    c. Available amounts
    d. Force-out eligible
    e. Hardship amounts
    f. Required Minimum Distribution amounts (Age 70½)
    g. Tax withholding
    h. Defaulted participant loans
    i. In-service
    j. Early retirement (Pre-retirement)
    k. Normal retirement
    l. Qualified Domestic Relations Order (QDRO)
    m. Installments, lump sum, partial, in-kind, cash, annuity
    n. Rollover
    o. Employer stock diversification
    p. Partial plan termination
    q. Plan termination

17. Earnings Allocations:

    a. Pooled accounts
    b. Self-directed accounts
    c. Participant
    d. Source (i.e. deferral, match, rollover, profit sharing, safe harbor, Roth, etc.)

18. Use of Forfeitures:

    a. Pay plan expenses
    b. Reduce employer contributions
    c. As an additional employer contribution
    d. Reinstate rehired participant previous forfeited amounts

19. Compliance testing (see *Chapter 12, Testing Matters*).

20. Plan filing deadlines (see *Chapter 4, Don't Miss Deadlines*).

401(k) ESSENTIALS FOR THE HR PROFESSIONAL

ESSENTIALS EXERCISE 11

Answer the following as they relate to your plan.

Four terms from the listings in this chapter you need to research are:

_____   _____

_____   _____

Who is determining when employees are eligible for the plan initially?
- ☐ In-house
  - ○ Payroll Department
  - ○ HR department
  - ○ Other : _____
- ☐ TPA
- ☐ Recordkeeper
- ☐ Payroll company
- ☐ Other: _____

What entity does your 401(k) trust accounting?
- ☐ In-house
  - ○ Payroll Department
  - ○ HR department
  - ○ Other : _____
- ☐ TPA
- ☐ Recordkeeper
- ☐ Payroll company
- ☐ Other: _____

The definition of compensation for the plan is:

_____

Does your Payroll department know the plan's definition of compensation?
- ☐ Yes
- ☐ No

Chapter 12

TESTING MATTERS

Compliance testing generally consists of making sure the plan isn't favoring a certain group of employees over the rest of the employees. The IRS regulations set standards for non-discrimination within a plan. To ensure the plan remains "qualified", compliance testing and passing the tests are vital.

Testing is essential to the plan retaining its "qualified" status. It is complicated, so this chapter is a bit advanced. However, you must be aware of these requirements. This core area is one very important reason to have a reputable TPA assisting you in performing these tests.

What Is Compliance Testing?

You've probably heard the terms "ADP testing" and "ACP testing". These key compliance tests are thought to be the most important tests for 401(k) plans. They relate to a participant's 401(k) deferrals and the company match.

There are other tests that must be met each year which are just as important to ensure the plan retains its qualified status.

The following is a list of compliance tests with the IRC section. Your TPA will assist you annually in performing these complex tests.

- Actual Deferral Percentage test (ADP)   IRC 401(k)
- Actual Contribution Percentage test (ACP) IRC 401(m)
- Top-heavy testing   IRC 417
- Minimum coverage testing   IRC 410(b)
- Comparable benefits test   IRC 401(a)(4)

IRC = Internal Revenue Code section

What Is ADP Testing?

Each year a 401(k) plan must perform an Actual Deferral Percentage (ADP) test as of the last day of the plan year. The purpose of the test is to confirm that Highly Compensated Employees (HCEs) do not contribute disproportionately more to the plan than Non-highly Compensated Employees (NHCEs). *Chapter 5, Employee Categories* helps explain who HCEs, NHCEs and Key Employees are. Be sure you know who your HCE and Key Employees are.

In simple terms, ADP testing ensures the HCEs are not deferring more from their pay, on average, than the average deferrals of the NHCEs as a group.

How do we determine these averages? Take the amount of deferral for each employee and express it as a percentage of their compensation. Add up the percentages and then divide by the number of employees in the group, being sure to include those who choose not to defer in this group. IRS regulations define how the averages are allowed to differ. You apply the test and determine if it produces a "pass" or a "fail".

If the plan "fails" this test, it must correct the failure by returning (distributing from the plan) the excess 401(k) deferrals to the affected HCEs. There are several other ways to correct a failure; however refunds are the most frequently used method for correcting a failed ADP test.

If your plan allows employees age 50 and older to contribute catch-up deferrals, the catch-up deferrals made during the plan year after applying 401(k) deferral limits and other plan limits are not included in the ADP test. This alone may cause the plan to "pass" the test without having to make refunds.

Your TPA knows the intricacies of this test and will assist you in applying it and making corrections if needed.

What Is ACP Testing?

If your company makes matching contributions for the plan year, the plan must perform the Actual Contribution Percentage (ACP) test as of the last day of the plan year. It works similarly to the ADP test.

You group the employees into 2 groups - HCEs and NHCEs. Determine the average of each group and test them against each other using the parameters set by IRS.

The source of the funds (dollars) being tested in the ACP test originated from employer contributions, unlike deferrals that are employee contributions.

If the plan "fails" this test, the most common method to correct the failure is by returning the "excess aggregate contributions". That is fancy language for returning a portion of the match made to certain HCEs.

ADP And ACP Testing Pointers

These tests can be complicated. There are nuances to the tests and every plan has a different set of factors that go into the testing. You should rely upon your TPA for assistance in performing these tests each year. A priority of the plan is to keep its qualified tax deferred status intact. Do not jeopardize this testing. It is one of the most important requirements of a 401(k) plan.

Provide your TPA with accurate data needed to perform these tests. Provide the data promptly. If the plan fails testing, corrections must be made within 2½ months after the end of the plan year in order to avoid an excise tax penalty. If you do not correct within that window, you will be required to file an IRS Form 5330 and submit the accompanying penalty tax. This form has a filing deadline similar to Form 5500. Be careful because there are penalties related to filing these forms late as well.

The return of contributions derived from the failure of these tests results in taxable income to the affected HCE (participant). The participant will receive a Form 1099-R in the following year. The amount reflected on the Form 1099-R will be included in their income on their personal tax returns.

For example, an HCE is required to receive a corrective refund of $1,000. It is related to the testing of the 2015 plan year. The refund is made in February 2016. The participant will receive his 2016 Form 1099-R in January 2017. The amount is taxable for the 2016 year.

When these corrections are made the regulations also require that the investment gains or losses attributable to these funds are distributed and included on the Form 1099-R. Your TPA will calculate the attributable investment gains or losses.

If your plan is a safe harbor 401(k) plan, the contributions your company makes to the plan should relieve you from having to perform the ADP and ACP tests. However, if your company contributes any additional matching funds above the safe harbor contribution, you may be subject to ACP testing. Check with your TPA if you are considering making an additional match above the safe harbor requirement.

What Is Top-Heavy Testing?

Top-heavy testing relates to how many total dollars in the plan are attributable to the "Key" employees. Key Employees and Highly Compensated Employees may not be the same. They are defined differently in the Internal Revenue Code.

Each year you need to determine if the plan is deemed top-heavy. If the 401(k) plan is not top-heavy but is nearing the level of becoming so, you must take action immediately to understand the financial impact it may have on your company. This is critical. Your TPA generally performs the top-heavy testing. Be sure to review the results each year.

A top-heavy test is performed at the end of each plan year. The results are then applied to the following year.

For example, to determine if a calendar year plan is top-heavy for 2016, the determination date is December 31, 2015. Therefore, the December 31, 2015 account balance for any participant who worked during 2015 is used to determine if the plan is top-heavy for 2016.

For a 401(k) plan to be top-heavy, the aggregate account balances of Key Employees must exceed 60% of total account balances of the Keys and Non-keys.

If (1) the test indicates the plan is top-heavy for 2016 and (2) a Key Employee receives an employer allocation during 2016 or makes 401(k) deferrals in 2016, the Non-key employees who are employed on December 31, 2016 <u>must</u> receive a minimum top-heavy allocation. <u>This means the employer will have to make contributions</u>.

CAUTION! This could be very costly to the company.

If the plan is top-heavy, what is the impact to the plan? The IRS requires:

1. An accelerated vesting schedule (at least three-year cliff or six- year graded); and
2. Minimum employer contributions of 3% to Non-keys.

The test and method of compliance have their own nuances. Again, have your TPA perform the actual testing.

What Is Coverage Testing?

Coverage testing was designed to ensure the plan is offered to different groups of employees and not just the HCEs or owners of the company.

This test uses comparative groups, HCEs versus NHCEs. Coverage testing looks at who is eligible, who is eligible but excluded from the plan, and who is receiving a benefit from the plan. Benefiting and participating are not the same thing. In a 401(k) plan an eligible employee (a participant) who chooses not to defer is still deemed to be benefiting in the plan by virtue of the fact they are offered participation in the plan.

The percentage of NHCEs benefiting under the plan must be at least 70% of the percentage of HCEs who benefit under the plan. This is called the Ratio Percentage Test. If the plan does not pass this test, it must pass the more complex Average Benefits Test. The plan must pass one of these tests on either a daily basis, a quarterly basis, or on an annual basis as of the last day of the plan year.

The 401(k) deferral, the match, and the profit sharing portions of a plan each must meet the minimum coverage requirement on an annual basis as of the last day of the plan year. You might ask, "Why aren't they the same?" Maybe your plan requires an employee to work a minimum number of hours to receive the profit sharing contribution, but the match does not have this minimum hours requirement. The employee groups for each type of contribution may not mirror each other. Therefore, the employee may be "benefiting" in receiving the match but not benefiting in the profit sharing component. So, the percentage of employees receiving a match may be different than the percentage receiving a profit sharing contribution.

Some plans only have to perform minimum coverage testing every three years. However, every third year when you test and pass coverage testing, the plan will then have to be able to demonstrate there were no significant changes in the preceding two plan years. Significant changes might include changes in plan provisions, the employer's workforce, or compensation practices.

A special transition rule allows plans involved in company level merger and acquisition situations to be treated as satisfying the minimum coverage requirements during a transition period following the transaction.

If you offer an additional qualified retirement plan to your employees, this area becomes very complex. Your TPA must be aware of the other plan's existence even if they don't administer the other plan.

TESTING MATTERS

Answer the following as they relate to your plan.

ESSENTIALS EXERCISE 12

Is your plan a safe harbor 401(k) plan?
- ☐ Yes
- ☐ No

Did your plan pass the ADP test last year?
- ☐ Yes
- ☐ No

Did the plan have to make refunds to any HCEs?
- ☐ Yes
- ☐ No

Were the refunds done timely?
- ☐ Yes
- ☐ No

If the plan failed the ADP test, have you done anything to encourage the NHCEs to defer more?
- ☐ Yes, describe: _____
- ☐ No (why not?): _____

Do you make matching contributions to the plan?
- ☐ Yes, and the matching formula is: _____
- ☐ No

If yes, did you pass the ACP test last year?
- ☐ Yes
- ☐ No

Is your plan top-heavy?
- ☐ Yes
- ☐ No

What percentage of the participant accounts belong to the Key Employees? _____

Is your vesting schedule top-heavy compliant?
- ☐ Yes, our vesting schedule is: _____
- ☐ No

Do you exclude any employees from the plan?
- ☐ Yes
- ☐ No

What provision in the plan document details these exclusions? _____

Chapter 13

PLAN DATA EXPLAINED

The foundation of 401(k) plan administration and testing must be based upon complete and accurate data. Data is defined as factual information, especially information organized for analysis or used to reason or make decisions. As reviewed in our earlier material (*Chapter 11, Determinations and Calculations*), all types of data are used for determinations and calculations. It is important to understand the types of data which will be gathered for the plan.

The results of calculations are only as reliable as the data provided.

What Data Is Essential To Your Plan?

There are three areas from which you will compile data:

- Employer
- Employee
- Investment

Complete and accurate data is essential to plan administration. Data is what the plan's qualification or potential disqualification will be based upon. Your TPA and CPA rely upon you to gather and provide the necessary data. The IRS and DOL require you to maintain the records.

Accuracy Is Key

Something as simple as an incorrect date will cause major issues with the plan. For example, a date of hire will determine when an employee is eligible. It could affect the determination of when they are eligible to enter the plan and if they will receive a contribution. It may be considered in determining when they might retire or when they will be fully vested.

Be sure to double check all information you compile and submit. When submitting payroll and 401(k) deferral information, make sure the totals on the payroll reports match the confirmations received by the investment company. When remitting the annual census to your TPA, make sure the totals tie to other proofing reports. Do the total compensation figures on the Form W-2s match those on the year-end payroll register? Do the total 401(k) deferrals match on these reports? Does the investment company report reflect the same total of 401(k) deferrals being received?

Make sure your TPA and your payroll system have correct and complete employee dates entered (dates of birth, hire, re-hire, termination, etc.).

What Employer Data Is Required By Your Plan?

The plan document and government reporting require the legal information of the plan sponsor (employer). If any of this data were to change, it would affect the plan's reporting, contracts, and the government's ability to match previous records, to name a few. Here is a short list of the data needed:

1. Legal name of plan sponsor (and adopting entities).
2. Mailing address.
3. Physical address.
4. Telephone number and fax number.
5. Employer's Tax Identification Number (EIN).
6. Fiscal year of employer.
7. Plan year anniversary date.

PLAN DATA EXPLAINED

8. Date plan sponsor began business.

9. Officers of the plan sponsor (entity).

10. Ownership information (individual's or entities who own 2% or more of the business).

11. Type of business entity (Corporation - including type, Partnership - including type, Sole Proprietorship, etc.).

12. Name of plan trustees.

13. Name and address of company's law firm (or attorney).

14. Name, address, and EIN of company's accounting firm (or CPA).

15. Employer's designated representative who will sign the Form 5500 for the plan (contact's name, telephone number, fax number, and email address).

16. Description of employer's business and/or business tax code describing entity.

17. Sale or purchase of any business.

What Employee Data Is Required By Your Plan?

In order to operate and administer the plan properly, employee data is crucial. Retirement benefits are related to age, service, and compensation paid by the employer. Calculation of contributions is related to compensation paid, hours worked and possibly years of service and age. Certain government reporting forms related to the plan require the social security number of employees.

Each year you will need to be prepared to report the following (or any changes) for each and every employee who worked at least one hour during the plan year:

1. Employee's full legal name.
2. Social Security Number (SSN).
3. Gender.
4. Employee number you assigned (if requested or needed).
5. Date of hire and re-hire (DOH).
6. Date of birth (DOB).
7. Date of separation from service (termination, death, disability, retirement), aka date of termination (DOT).
8. Actual hours worked or credited for the year.
9. Compensation paid for the year (see your plan document).
10. 401(k) deferral amount.
11. Matching contribution amount.
12. Change in beneficiary designation.

What Investment Data Is Required By Your Plan?

The plan is required to report the value of the plan's investment holdings each year. Therefore, you need an annual summary of the plan's asset holdings. The report should include an aggregate listing of all employees' accounts and individual employee account details, too.

Here is a list of what you may need:

1. List of assets held at the end of the year with fair market value by asset as of the year-end date.
2. A list of all participant loans which includes the opening and ending balances, interest paid, principal paid, default amount, interest rate, and term of loan.

PLAN DATA EXPLAINED

3. An income and expense summary for the plan year with detail (contributions, interest, dividends, gains and losses, expenses, etc.).

4. List of distributions paid to participants during the plan year.

5. List of contributions made by type (401(k) deferral, Roth, match, rollover, etc.) including date withheld, date transmitted or deposited and the amount.

6. Commissions and expenses paid to brokers, investment company(s), mutual funds, etc.

7. Fees paid by plan to service providers.

What Is The Annual Data Used For?

This annual data is used for the administration, compliance, and government reporting of the plan.

- ➢ Employer Data - used on government forms and plan reports

- ➢ Employee Data - used for calculations, compliance testing, government reporting, and plan reports

- ➢ Investment Data - used for calculations, compliance testing, government reporting, and plan reports

Did You Know You Must Ensure All Of This Data Is Gathered And Provided To Your TPA?

It is important that your 401(k) team work together in gathering, processing, and reporting this information as required. While you may have been led to believe there is nothing you need to do, now you can see that is not true. You may have data others do not. Understand the requirements to make the data gathering go smoothly each year.

ESSENTIALS EXERCISE 13

Answer the following as they relate to your plan.

Who is responsible for providing your TPA with the annual employee census information? _____

Explain how this data is verified and checked before it is sent to the TPA:
_____
_____

Are 401(k) deferral deposits verified between the payroll report and the investment company report to ensure each deposit matches?
- ☐ Yes
- ☐ No

Who is approving the match calculations on a per-pay-period basis?
_____

Do you know how to obtain a listing of outstanding participant loan balances as of the end of the plan year?
- ☐ Yes
- ☐ No

On a scale of 1 (being least confident) and 10 (being extremely confident), what is your level of confidence in the accuracy of the census data you provide the TPA each year? _____

What employee data might be the least accurately reported?
- ☐ Social Security Numbers
- ☐ Dates of Birth
- ☐ Dates of Hire
- ☐ Dates of Termination

PLAN DATA EXPLAINED

When was the last time you had the above information confirmed by each employee? _____

What steps will you take to improve the accuracy of the data? _____

_____

_____

Chapter 14

RECORD RETENTION COUNTS

When you are subject to Internal Revenue Service scrutiny, you must be able to substantiate your reporting. Since your 401(k) plan is subject to IRS regulations, it is vital that you maintain records for the plan.

The 401(k) plan has many facets and therefore requires a tremendous amount of documentation. As the plan sponsor, you are required to store and/or have access to all plan information.

Establish A Record Retention Policy

When establishing the policy, be sure it includes instruction on handling paper and electronic versions of the records.

The policy should include how to handle documents, transactions, correspondence, etc. As we strive to become a paperless society, be sure to address how to handle email communications and correspondence, including 401(k) plan communications internally and externally. Establishing a "Dropbox" or "Cloud" storage to maintain emails might ease the pressure for the various parties in following the policy.

Records must be kept in a format or way that they can be readily retrieved. If the records are lost, stolen or destroyed before the expiration of the retention period, you will be required to recreate the records. The only exception is if doing so will result in excessive or unreasonable costs.

Periodically review your policy. Continue to refine the policy to ensure you update, protect, and dispose of documents in a thought out and organized manner to meet plan compliance standards and requirements. Make sure the policy strives to make easy retrieval a priority.

Why Have A Policy?

We live in a litigious society. You never know when a disgruntled employee might make a claim to the Department of Labor. Even a divorce of a participant could create a hostile situation.

Fiduciary standards are becoming more prevalent. You will need to be able to prove plan compliance and have immediate access to necessary records.

Who Might Request Information?

Because qualified plans are regulated by three governmental agencies, the DOL, IRS, and Pension Benefit Guaranty Corporation (PBGC), you should be prepared to receive inquiries from each of these agencies. Routine government audits are increasingly commonplace. If a plan's records are not complete and orderly, such investigations can turn into a confusing and expensive ordeal for you. Any governmental inquiry can be resolved quickly, without interruption to normal business and without sanction to the plan or the plan sponsor, if complete and accurate records are kept.

Participants may request information. Upon the written request from a participant or beneficiary, the Plan Administrator must provide a copy of any of the following requested items:

> - the latest updated SPD, including any SMMs
>
> - the plan's latest annual report (Form 5500)
>
> - the plan document, collective bargaining agreement, trust agreement, contracts, or other instruments under which the plan is established or operated

Be prepared!

How Long Must You Retain Plan Records?

The short answer is for six years after the filing date of the plan's government filings, such as a Form 5500. However, you are complying with IRS regulations, so there are nuances to this rule. Consider keeping certain records for the life of the plan. This should include all plan documents dating from the plan's inception.

The more information you have available, the less problematic it will be to respond to an inquiry, whether from the government or a request for information from a participant.

Who Must Retain The Plan Records?

ERISA (the regulations) requires the Plan Administrator (employer/plan sponsor) retain records and the Department of Labor requires records to substantiate the participant's benefit in the plan be maintained. Do not rely upon your TPA, advisors, and service providers. Record retention is your responsibility. Make it a priority. These companies may not be associated with the plan in five years.

What Plan Records Are Important?

ERISA required documents include the following:

1. The original signed and dated plan document and subsequent restatements, plus all signed and dated plan amendments. Make sure the dates and signatures are present on restatements, adoption agreements, master documents, and amendments.

2. Copies of all corporate/partnership actions relating to the 401(k) plan and administrative committee actions relating to the plan.

3. Copies of all communications to employees and participants; including the Summary Plan Descriptions, Summary of Material

Modifications, and anything else provided to the participants describing the plan. Be sure to keep copies of correspondence (emails, memos, letters, etc.), enrollment kits, videos, slide shows, and other important communications.

4. A copy of the most recent favorable determination letter from the IRS, or the form to request that determination letter, if one is pending. To take it a step further, keep all past copies as well.

5. All financial reports, including balance sheets, income and expense statements, trustees' reports, transactions, certified audits, and investment analyses.

6. Copies of Form 5500 and related schedules, attachments, and extensions.

7. Payroll records used to determine eligibility and contributions. The details supporting any exclusion from participation are equally important. Census data is vital to the plan operation and compliance. It is crucial to keep complete census data, not just data on those who are eligible.

8. Employee hours of service.

9. Vesting computations.

10. Plan distribution records which include the Form 1099-R.

11. Corporate, partnership, or business income tax returns reflecting the contribution deductions.

12. Copy of the plan's fidelity bond.

13. Documentation supporting the trust's ownership of the plan's assets.

14. Copies of all documents relating to plan loans, distributions, and withdrawals, including copies of spousal consents which were required at the time.

15. Copies of all nondiscrimination and coverage test results (i.e. ADP and ACP tests, top-heavy tests, comparable benefits, and so on).

16. Any other plan related materials, such as claims against the plan.

17. Corporate action items taken to adopt the plan or make amendments require easily visible dates and signatures.

18. Copies of all correspondence to and from the service providers.

19. Copies of any IRS correspondence relating to the plan.

As noted above, generally, these documents should be kept for a period of six years after the date of the filing to which they relate.

Plan Records - Paper Versus Electronic?

According to the Department of Labor, electronic media may be used for purposes of complying with the record retention requirements, if the following requirements are met:

- The recordkeeping system has reasonable controls to ensure the accuracy of the records.

- The recordkeeping system is capable of indexing, retaining, preserving, retrieving, and reproducing the electronic records. Be careful as technology changes. If records are on floppy disks and you no longer have equipment that can read the data, you will be unable to provide it.

- The electronic records can be easily converted into legible paper copies.

- The electronic recordkeeping system is not subject to restrictions that would inappropriately limit access to the records.

Once you have transferred the paper records to electronic versions, you may dispose of them provided the recordkeeping system complies with the above requirements.

CAUTION! Don't discard an original if it has legal significance or some value in its original form (e.g., notarized documents, contracts, stock certificates, and documents executed under seal).

RECORD RETENTION COUNTS

Answer the following as they relate to your plan.

ESSENTIALS
EXERCISE 14

Are you adhering to the record retention requirement?
- ☐ Yes
- ☐ No

Where are the copies of your original plan documents stored? _____

When was the last time you sent a memo to your staff about plan records retention? How often do you communicate electronically with your service providers and remember to record these communications in the plan files pursuant to your Record Retention Policy?
- ☐ Never
- ☐ Annually
- ☐ Periodically

Are you confident that you could produce information requested by the IRS in a reasonable amount of time?
- ☐ Yes
- ☐ No

Does your IT department understand the importance of backing up these confidential files?
- ☐ Yes
- ☐ No

Do your 401(k) plan files contain a copy of the annual payroll registers for the last six years?
- ☐ Yes
- ☐ No

If you have a secure intranet where you place plan documentation, is there a record of what you've provided to the employees on the site?
- ☐ Yes
- ☐ No

Chapter 15

MISTAKES HAPPEN

Remember the phrase, "I never met a person that..."? Most pension professionals haven't met a plan that hasn't encountered a problem. Mistakes happen.

Keeping your plan qualified is imperative. However, there may be times when you made a mistake, missed a deadline or omitted information that you didn't realize was necessary. The IRS recognizes that mistakes happen.

The IRS has established procedures for correcting administrative mistakes. They also have created formal programs to allow a plan to pay a penalty, correct the error, and maintain the plan's qualified status.

How Do You Know What To Do With All These Complicated Tests, Filings, And Reports?

Make sure you understand the roles of your 401(k) team members. Surround yourself with experts.

Know your plan's provisions, policies, and procedures. Ask questions.

Attend training.

Implement internal controls, especially within your benefits department and the payroll department. Having controls in place can:

> Eliminate or reduce errors in plan operation

> Help quickly identify errors to correct via the IRS Self-Correction process with minimal cost

- Help positively impact the IRS Audit Closing Agreement Program (Audit CAP) sanction negotiations

- Keep an audit "focused"

- Significantly reduce the time for conducting an examination or audit

- Shorten turnaround time on request for further information during the examination or audit

- Promote clear communication between the IRS, the plan sponsor, and service providers

List Of Common Mistakes Recently Published By IRS

1. Failing to amend plan document promptly.

2. Failing to follow the terms of your plan document.

3. Using incorrect compensation for your employees (see your plan's definition of compensation).

4. Not calculating the matching contributions correctly.

5. Omitting eligible employees.

6. Loan problems.

7. Nondiscrimination testing (ADP and ACP) errors.

8. Employees exceeding the 401(k) annual dollar limit.

9. Not making timely deposits of employee elective deferrals.

10. Hardship distribution problems.

Knowing what mistakes others have made should assist you in learning what mistakes NOT to make.

MISTAKES HAPPEN

IRS Offers Correction Programs

When mistakes are made, correct them immediately. Understand what the correction is to be, if there is a penalty, if the situation needs to be reported, and which IRS correction program is available for the situation.

Learn from the mistake. Implement standards and controls that will prevent it from happening again. Create a new plan policy to document what you've done to fix, correct, and prevent mistakes.

Currently, the IRS has three correction programs:
- SCP - Self Correction Program
- VCP - Voluntary Compliance Program
- Audit CAP - Audit Closing Agreement Program

And, the Department of Labor's program is:
- DFVCP - Delinquent Filer Voluntary Correction Program

IRS Provides Volumes Of Information On The Web To Educate And Assist You With Understanding 401(k) Plan Operation

Check out the IRS website devoted to retirement plans.

www.irs.gov/Retirement-Plans

Here's a brief list of things you will find on the IRS site:

- Information to assist you in understanding the formal correction programs

- The IRS has published a document to assist in preventing errors called *The 401(k) Checklist*. Download, review, and implement it. There is an excerpt in *Appendix D* at the back of this book.

- Employee Plans Compliance Resolution System (EPCRS) - Check out the information

- Employee Plans newsletter - Subscribe today.

- Phone Forum programs - You should participate.

- Fact Sheets - Review them.

- FAQs – Review and check back to see if there are new ones.

- Publications, videos and booklets on specific topics - Browse and download.

- Guides - Browse and download.

- News - Keep current with the news.

Department Of Labor's EFAST Website Also Provides Important Information

Check out the links available on their website which is full of informative materials:

www.dol.gov/ebsa

How To Avoid Mistakes

- Ask questions

- Understand your plan

- Implement policies and procedures

- Service providers are available to you to be of assistance

- Create a plan task and deadline calendar. There are sample calendars and checklists in the Appendices at the back of this book.

- Meet with your internal departments (such as payroll) quarterly to check in on their role and performance of duties related to the 401(k) plan

- Subscribe to the IRS, DOL and EFAST websites

- Develop and implement internal controls

- Take control of the plan

- Double check the data you provide to the service providers

- Don't stress

- Educate your fiduciaries on their responsibilities

- Educate your plan participants periodically

- Continue to keep abreast of plan developments

- Talk to your peers about their plans

How Will You Know If There Is A Mistake?

Ask questions before you do something. This is especially true if it has to do with money coming into the plan or leaving the plan.

Your TPA should review your plan annually and advise you if something is not correct, missing, or appears unclear.

Periodically refer to this book to continue building your knowledge of operating a 401(k) plan.

And, finally - **Know Your Plan!**

ESSENTIALS EXERCISE 15

Answer the following as they relate to your plan.

Do you have 401(k) internal controls?
☐ Yes (Good job)
☐ No (Caution)

Are the controls written and understood by the parties involved?
☐ Yes (Good job)
☐ No (Begin now)

How often do you review these controls? _____

Visit the IRS website today and subscribe to the IRS newsletter while on their website: **www.irs.gov/Retirement-Plans**

Visit the EFAST website today: **www.efast.dol.gov**

Have you reviewed your plan's Participant Loan Policy to ensure you understand it?
☐ Yes
☐ No

Are you certain you are administering your participant loans in accordance with the Loan Policy? Maybe be you should check.
☐ Yes
☐ No

Have any of your participants taken hardship distributions this year?
☐ Yes
☐ No

Have you confirmed with payroll when each six month cessation period will expire for participants who took hardship distributions?
☐ Yes
☐ No

APPENDICES

Appendix A

STEPS IN ESTABLISHING A 401(k) PLAN

Step	1	Engage a Plan Administrator (TPA)
Step	2	Engage a Financial Advisor for the Plan
Step	3	Select and Design Plan and its Parameters
Step	4	Determine Plan Trustees
Step	5	Create Legal Plan Document
Step	6	Create Summary Plan Description
Step	7	Create Board Resolution Approving Adoption of said Plan
Step	8	Request an EIN for the Plan's Trust from IRS
Step	9	Select Investment Company and/or Fund Choices
Step	10	Sign All Documents and Contracts
Step	11	Distribute Summary Plan Description
Step	12	Distribute Required Plan Notices (ie. Safe Harbor)
Step	13	Schedule Employee Enrollment Meetings
Step	14	Market the Plan to Employees
Step	15	Obtain Enrollment Kits from Investment Provider
Step	16	Conduct Enrollment Meetings and Provide Investment Company with Employee Fund Allocations
Step	17	Implement Procedures with Payroll to Effectuate the Deduction of the Deferrals
Step	18	Determine Matching Contribution Associated with Deferrals, if applicable
Step	19	Implement Procedures to Transmit Dollars to the Investment Company
Step	20	Review Plan Sponsors Duties
Step	21	Appoint Internal Liason / Plan Contact for Participants, TPA, Financial Advisor and Investment Company
Step	22	Start Deferrals
Step	23	Remit Deferrals
Step	24	Create and Maintain 401(k) Plan Files for Easy Access
Step	25	Understand Plan Deadlines and Calendar Them to Avoid Penalties and Balance Workload
Step	26	Understand what Information must be Collected for Year End Compliance Tasks
Step	27	If Plan Is Deemed a Large Plan (100+ Participants), engage CPA Firm for Required Audit for Form 5500
Step	28	Obtain Electronic Filing Credential from EFAST2 for Signing and Filing Annual Form 5500
Step	29	Obtain the Plan's Required Fiduciary Bond
Step	30	Obtain Forms for Future use to have on hand from Investment Company and TPA

Appendix B

SETTING UP THE PLAN SPONSOR'S 401(k) FILES

I. Plan Document (3-ring binder suggested)

1. Resolutions
2. Amendments
3. Policies and Procedures
   a. Loan
   b. Distribution
   c. QDRO
   d. Investment
   e. Other
4. Adoption Agreement and/or Plan Document
5. Summary Plan Description (SPD) and Summary Material Modifications (SMM)
6. Any Correspondence relating to the document
7. Government Forms [SS-4, 5307, etc.]
8. Fidelity Bond
9. Other

II. Annual Administration files for each plan year (keep most recent 7 years)

1. Each Plan Year Administration
   - Admin package as it was delivered to you from TPA
   - Annual Investment Summary Report from investment company/record keeper
   - Census Data provided to TPA
     - Including backup from which data was taken
     - Annual Payroll register
     - W-2s
   - Annual Testing
     - ADP/ACP
     - Top Heavy
     - Coverage
   - Resolution outlining any Employer Contributions
     - Match
     - Safe Harbor
     - Profit Sharing
   - TPAs annual questionnaire completed as sent
   - Year End Participant Loan Summary
   - Listing of any Hardship distributions made and the date the 6 month restriction will expire on each

2. Government Forms
   - Form 5500
   - Form 8955-SSA
   - Form 1099-R
   - Form 1096
   - Form 945
   - Form 5330
   - EBSA Electronic Signature data and password
   - Other

3. Participant Communications
   - Annual Notices
   - Memos distributing forms or information

SETTING UP THE PLAN SPONSOR'S 401(k) FILES

- Letters from or regarding participants
- QDROs
- Request for Information
- Hardship Backup

4. Correspondence
   - TPA
   - Record keeper
   - CPA
   - Auditors
   - IRS
   - other

III. Loans and Distribution Binders

1. Loan Documents
   a. Promissory Note with signatures
   b. Amortization Schedule
   c. Loan Application
   d. Notification of Payment Schedule provided to payroll department

2. Distribution Forms
   a. Current year Distributions to terminated participants
   b. Hardship Withdrawal
   c. In-service Withdrawal (if permitted)
   d. Age 70-1/2 (RMDs)
   e. Defaulted Loans
   f. Death Benefits with death certificate and beneficiary designation
   g. Disability Benefits with substantiating documentation
   h. QDRO and Alternate Payee Election forms

IV. Beneficiary Forms

V. Other Files

1. Plan Contacts List (name, title, role, email, company, address, telephone, fax, etc.)
2. Billing Folder
3. Pending Projects
4. Board of Directors and management communications
5. Employee Forms

   - Enrollment
   - SPD/SMM
   - SAR
   - Beneficiary Designation
   - Deferral Change Form
   - Loan Application and Policy
   - Distribution Forms
   - QDRO Procedure

6. Electronic files of all the above
7. Plan statistics
8. Industry trends

Appendix C

401(k) Resource Guide - Plan Sponsors - Filing Requirements

The plan sponsor is responsible for ensuring that its plan operates in compliance with the rules related to qualified plans. The plan sponsor is also subject to certain filing requirements. A list of those requirements is included here. Penalties may apply for the late filing or non-filing of required returns and reports.

This checklist may be used as a tool to help you meet 401(k) filing requirements. Please see the instructions to the applicable forms or the references for detailed information. **This checklist is not intended to be all-inclusive.**

Required to be file when applicable:

Item	Explanation	Due to:
Form 945, Annual Return of Withheld Federal Income Tax	Used to report income tax withheld from distributions made from qualified plans. Deposits of the tax with a Form 8109 to an authorized depositary must be made at specified times during the tax year.	IRS: By January 31st of the year following the calendar year in which the distribution was made.
Form 990-T, Exempt Organization Business Income Tax Return	Used to report gross unrelated business income of $1,000 or more. Generally deposits of the tax with a Form 8109 to an authorized depositary must be made at specified times during the tax year.	IRS: By the 15th day of the 4th month after the end of the tax year.
Form 1099-R, Distributions From Pensions, Annuities, Retirement or Profit-Sharing Plans, IRAs, Insurance Contracts, etc.	Used to report distributions, including direct rollovers, from qualified plans.	Participant: by January 31st following the calendar year of the distribution. IRS: By February 28th of the year following the calendar year of the distribution.
Form 5310-A, Notice of Plan Merger or Consolidation, Spinoff or Transfer of Plan Assets or Liabilities; Notice of Qualified Separate Lines of Business (QSLOB)	Used to inform the IRS of plan merger or consolidation, spinoff or transfer of plan assets or liabilities, or QSLOB.	IRS: At least 30 days prior to plan merger, consolidation, spinoff or transfer of plan assets to another employer. For QSLOB: By the later of October 15th of the year following the testing year, or the 15th day of the 10th month after the end of the plan year of the plan of the employer that begins earliest in the testing year.
Form 5329, Additional Taxes on Qualified Plans (Including IRAs) and Other Tax-Favored Accounts	Used to report and pay additional taxes.	IRS: As an attachment to the Individual Income Tax Return. (Note: filed by participant)
Form 5330, Return of Excise Taxes Related to Employee Benefit Plans	Used to report tax on the following IRC sections: 4971 - minimum funding deficiency 4972 - nondeductible contributions to qualified plans 4973(a)(3) - excess contributions to a 403(b)(7) custodial account 4975 - prohibited transactions 4978, 4978A - certain ESOP dispositions 4979 - excess contributions to plans with cash or deferred arrangements 4979A - certain prohibited allocations of qualified securities by an ESOP 4980 - reversion of qualified plan assets to employers 4980F - failure of applicable plans reducing future benefit accruals to satisfy notice requirements	IRS: For taxes due under: 4971 - later of the last day of the 7th month after the end of the employer's tax year or 8 1/2 months after the last day of the plan year that ends with or within the filer's tax year. 4972, 4973(a)(3), 4975, 4978, 4978A, and 4979A - last day of the 7th month after the end of the tax year of the employer or other person who must file this return. 4979 - last day of the 15th month after the close of the plan year to which the excess contributions or excess aggregate contributions relate. 4980 - last day of the month following the month in which the reversion occurred. 4980F - last day of the month following the month in which the failure occurred.
Form 5558, Application for Extension of Time to File Certain Employee Plans Returns	Provides a 2 1/2 month extension to file the Form 5500 or 5500-EZ; a 6 month extension to file Form 5330.	IRS: By the last day of the 7th month after the end of the plan year for a 5500 extension; before otherwise due for a 5330 extension.
Form 5500, Annual Return/Report of Employee Benefit Plan or Form 5500-EZ, Annual Return of One-Participant (Owners and Their Spouses) Retirement Plan with applicable schedules and independent auditor's report, if applicable.	An administrator or sponsor of an employee benefit plan subject to ERISA must file information about each plan every year. A Form 5500-EZ may generally be filed for a plan that provides benefits solely for an individual (and spouse) who wholly owns a trade or business; or partners or partners (and spouses) in a partnership.	IRS/DOL: By the last day of 7th month after the end of the plan year.
Form W-2, Wage and Tax Statement	Reports wages and the amount of elective deferrals for a 401(k) plan.	Employees: By January 31st following the calendar year. IRS: by February 28th following the calendar year.

http://www.irs.gov/Retirement-Plans/Plan-Sponsor/401(k)-Resource-Guide---Plan-Sponsors---Filing-Requirements

Appendix D

401(k) Plan Checklist

This checklist isn't a complete description of all plan requirements, and shouldn't be used as a substitute for a complete plan review.

For Business Owner's Use

(DO NOT SEND THIS WORKSHEET TO THE IRS)

Every year it's important that you review the requirements for operating your 401(k) retirement plan. Use this checklist to help you keep your plan in compliance with many of the important rules. For additional information (including examples) on how to find, fix and avoid each mistake, click on "(More)." See www.irs.gov/retirement and click on "Types of Retirement Plans" for Fix-It Guides and other resources for 401(k) and other plan types.

1. Has your plan document been updated within the past few years? Yes No

If your plan hasn't been updated to reflect recent law changes, the plan needs to be revised.
(More)

2. Are the plan operations based on the plan document terms? Yes No

Failure to follow the terms of the plan is a common problem found on audit.
(More)

3. Is the plan definition of compensation for all deferrals and allocations used correctly? Yes No

Your plan may use different definitions of compensation for different purposes. It's important that you apply the proper definition found in your plan document.
(More)

4. Were employer matching contributions made to appropriate employees under the plan terms? Yes No

The plan terms must be followed when allocating employer matching contributions.
(More)

5. Has the plan satisfied the 401(k) ADP and ACP nondiscrimination tests? Yes No

Most 401(k) plans must satisfy yearly ADP/ACP nondiscrimination tests.
(More)

6. Were all eligible employees identified and given the opportunity to make an elective deferral? Yes No

By supplying your tax advisor with information regarding all employees who receive a Form W-2, you may reduce the risk of omitting eligible employees.
(More)

7. Are elective deferrals limited to the IRC Section 402(g) limits for the calendar year? Yes No

Failure to distribute deferrals in excess of the 402(g) limit may result in additional taxes and penalties to the participant and employer.
(More)

8. Have you timely deposited employee elective deferrals? Yes No

You should deposit deferrals as soon as they can be segregated from the employer's assets.
(More)

9. Do participant loans meet the plan document and IRC Section 72(p) requirements? Yes No

Defaulted loans or loans in violation of IRC Section 72(p) may be treated as a taxable distribution to the participant.
(More)

10. Were hardship distributions made properly? Yes No

If a plan allows hardship distributions, the plan terms must be followed.
(More)

11. Were top-heavy minimum contributions made? Yes No

If the plan is top-heavy, minimum contributions for non-key employees are required.
(More)

12. Was Form 5500 filed? Yes No

Many 401(k) plans must make an annual filing with the Federal government.
(More)

If you answered "No" to any of the above questions, you may have made a mistake in the operation of your 401(k) plan. This list is only a guide to a more compliant plan, so answering "Yes" to each question may not mean your plan is 100% compliant. Many mistakes can be corrected easily, without penalty and without notifying the IRS.

■ contact your tax advisor   ■ www.irs.gov/retirement   ■ call the IRS at (877) 829-5500

Publication 4531 (Rev. 10-2014) Catalog Number 48552T Department of the Treasury **Internal Revenue Service** www.irs.gov

Appendix E

401(k) Plan Fix-It Guide

Mistake	Find the Mistake	Fix the Mistake	Avoid the Mistake
1) You haven't updated your plan document within the past few years to reflect recent law changes.	Review the annual cumulative list to see if the plan has all required law changes	Adopt amendments for missed law changes. If you missed the deadline to adopt an amendment you may need to use the IRS correction program.	Use a calendar that notes when you must complete amendments. Review your plan document annually. Maintain regular contact with the company that sold you the plan.
2) You didn't base the plan operations on the terms of the plan document. Failure to follow plan terms is a very common mistake.	Conduct an independent review of the plan document provisions compared to its operation.	Apply reasonable correction method that would place affected participants in the position they would've been in if there were no operational plan defects.	Develop a communication mechanism to make all relevant parties aware of changes on a timely and accurate basis (best practices). Perform a review at least annually to ensure that you're following plan terms.
3) You didn't use the plan definition of compensation correctly for all deferrals and allocations.	Review the plan document definition of compensation used for determining elective deferrals, employer nonelective and matching contributions, maximum annual additions and top-heavy minimum contributions. Review the plan election forms to determine if they're consistent with plan terms.	Corrective contribution or distribution.	Perform annual reviews of compensation definitions and ensure that the person in charge of determining compensation is properly trained to understand the plan document.
4) Employer matching contributions weren't made to all appropriate employees.	Review the plan document to determine the employee eligibility requirements and matching contribution formula. Compare it to what's used in operation.	Apply a reasonable correction method that would put affected participants in the same position they would've been in if there were no operational plan defects.	Contact plan administrators to ensure that they have adequate employment and payroll records to make calculations.
5) The plan failed the 401(k) ADP and ACP nondiscrimination tests.	Conduct an independent review to determine if highly and nonhighly employees are properly classified.	Make qualified nonelective contributions for the nonhighly compensated employees.	Consider a safe harbor or automatic enrollment plan design. Communicate with plan administrators to ensure proper employee classification and compliance with the plan terms.

401(k) Plan Fix-It Guide

Mistake	Find the Mistake	Fix the Mistake	Avoid the Mistake
6) Eligible employees weren't given the opportunity to make an elective deferral (exclusion of eligible employees).	Review the plan document sections on eligibility and participation. Check with plan administrators to determine when employees are entering the plan.	Make a qualified nonelective contribution for the employee that compensates for the missed deferral opportunity.	Monitor census information and apply participation requirements.
7) Elective deferrals weren't limited to the amounts under IRC Section 402(g) for the calendar year and excess deferrals weren't distributed.	Inspect deferral amounts for plan participants to ensure that the employee hasn't exceeded the limits.	Distribute excess deferrals.	Work with plan administrators to ensure that they have sufficient payroll information to verify the deferral limitations of IRC Section 402(g) were satisfied.
8) You haven't timely deposited employee elective deferrals.	Determine the earliest date you can segregate deferrals from general assets. Compare that date with the actual deposit date and any plan document requirements.	Usually corrected through DOL's Voluntary Fiduciary Correction Program. You may also need to correct through the IRS correction program. Deposit all elective deferrals withheld and earnings resulting from the late deposit into the plan's trust	Coordinate with your payroll provider to determine the earliest date you can reasonably segregate the deferral deposits from general assets. Set up procedures to ensure that you make deposits by that date.
9) Participant loans don't conform to the requirements of the plan document and IRC Section 72(p).	Review the plan document and all outstanding loans to ensure that the loans comply with the plan terms and that employees are repaying their loans timely.	You may correct some failures by corrective repayment and/or modification of loan terms.	Review and follow the plan provisions on loans, including the loan amount, term of the loan and repayment terms. Ensure that there are procedures in place to prevent loans that are prohibited transactions.
10) Hardship distributions weren't made properly.	Review all in-service distributions and determine whether hardship distributions met the plan requirements.	Amend plan retroactively to allow for hardship distributions. If impermissible hardship distribution, have participant return hardship distribution amount plus earnings.	Be familiar with your plan document's hardship provisions and ensure that you follow the provisions in operation. Ensure that your plan administrators and payroll offices share the plan's hardship distribution information.
11) The plan was top-heavy and required minimum contributions weren't made to the plan.	Review the rules and definitions for top-heavy found in your plan document. Determine whether your plan is top-heavy for the plan year.	Properly contribute and allocate the required top-heavy minimum, adjusted for earnings, to the affected non-key employees.	Perform a top-heavy test each year.

401(k) Plan Fix-It Guide

Mistake	Find the Mistake	Fix the Mistake	Avoid the Mistake
12) You haven't filed a Form 5500-series return this year.	Find your signed copy of the return and determine if you filed it timely.	File all delinquent returns.	Understand your filing requirement and know who filed and when. Don't assume someone else is taking care of it.

Appendix F

Frequently Asked Questions on EFAST2 Credentials

U.S. Department of Labor
Employee Benefits Security Administration
July 2012

Q1. Who needs to register to use EFAST2?

- Anyone wishing to complete the Form 5500 or Form 5500-SF and/or the schedules by using IFILE must register for author credentials. Check the "Filing Author" and/or "Schedule Author" user type(s) when registering.

- All plan sponsors, plan administrators, individuals signing for DFEs, and plan service providers which have written authorization to file on behalf of the plan administrator under the EFAST2 e-signature option must register for credentials to sign filings. Check the "Filing Signer" user type when registering. If an individual is signing a filing as the plan sponsor is the plan administrator, that individual only needs to register once.

- Anyone wishing to transmit completed filings through third party software may need to register for credentials and check the "Transmitter" user type. Check with your third party software provider to determine if this is necessary.

Enrolled actuaries and accountants do not need to register as a Filing Signer to manually sign Schedule SB, Schedule MB or an accountant's opinion and audit report filed with a Form 5500 or Form 5500-SF. Registration as a Filing Signer is required for individuals who will be electronically signing filings submitted to EFAST2. Upon registering, you will be issued the following credentials:

- User ID (used to identify you)
- PIN (used as your electronic signature)
- Password (allows you access to authorized EFAST2 Web site applications such as IFILE)

Although you provide employment information when registering, the credentials are personal and are not linked to a company or plan.

Access to the part of the EFAST2 Web site that provides basic public disclosure and reference information does not require registration.

Q2. How do I register for EFAST2 credentials?

Registration is performed on the EFAST2 Web site, select "Register" on the Welcome screen. You can get your EFAST2 credentials by completing seven easy steps. The whole process should take just a few minutes.

1. Read and accept the privacy statement.

2. On the next screen, provide contact information (name, address, phone, company name, etc.) and select one or more of the five user types. For example, someone preparing, signing, and submitting a filing through IFILE will choose "Filing Author" and "Filing Signer".

3. Select one of the two challenge (or security) questions and provide an answer. The challenge question and answer is used in case you forget your password.

4. After verifying that the information you entered is correct, you will see the Registration Confirmation screen telling you that completion of your registration will be pending until you receive your Credentials Notification email with further instructions. EFAST2 generates and sends the Credentials Notification email within five minutes.

5. Once you receive the Credentials Notification email, select the link in the email that will take you to a secure EFAST2 web site, which will ask you for the answer to your challenge (or security) question.

6. You will be asked to accept the PIN Agreement, which describes the security of your PIN and what to do if your PIN is lost or stolen. You will also be asked to accept the Signature Agreement if you will be signing the Form 5500 or Form 5500-SF.

7. You will be prompted to create a password. The password must be between 8 and 16 characters long and must not contain spaces. You must use at least one uppercase letter, one lower case letter at least one number and at least one of the following special characters [!, @, $, %, ^, &, *, (,)] No other special characters are allowed. Your new password must be different from your last 12 previous passwords. This field is case-sensitive and must be re-set after 90 days.

Once you have your UserID, PIN, and password, your EFAST2 registration is complete.

Q3. How long does it take to receive my Credentials Notification e-mail?

Within five minutes of submission and acceptance of the registration form, EFAST2 should generate the credentials. Once the credentials are generated, EFAST2 sends a notification to the email address provided during registration. In this e-mail notification, you will find a link to a secure Web site as well as instructions on how to retrieve and activate the credentials.

Q4. I did not receive my registration e-mail. What should I do?

If you did not receive the Credentials Notification email in your inbox within about five minutes, it may have been blocked as "spam" or "junk mail." Check your "spam" or "junk" email folders to see if you have received the email.

Some e-mail providers require that you add an email address to your address book before you can receive any email from that address. To ensure that our messages can be delivered to your inbox, enter into your address book both our originating email address, efast2@efastsys.dol.gov and our "reply to" e-mail address, **efast2@efast.dol.gov**.

If you checked your "spam" or "junk" e-mail folders and the email has not been received, you can complete the final registration steps using "Forgot User ID" on the **Login page**. After clicking "Forgot User ID," enter the email address that you entered during registration. If you have not completed the registration process, you will see an option to "Complete Registration" on the screen. Follow the instructions on the remaining screens to complete your registration.

Q5.   My account has been locked. What should I do?

To reset your locked account, from the EFAST2 Web site select "Login" on the Welcome screen, then select "Forgot Password." You will be prompted to enter either your User ID or your email address. Once you enter either your User ID or email address, you will then be prompted to answer your challenge question.

You will have three attempts to provide your challenge answer correctly before your user account is temporarily revoked for up to 20 minutes. After the allotted time, you may attempt to answer the challenge question again. If you repeatedly reach the limit of invalid challenge responses, your account may be permanently revoked. If that occurs, you will need to call the EFAST2 Help Desk at **1-866-GO-EFAST** (1-866-463-3278) or register again.

Q6.   I don't remember my User ID. How can I retrieve it?

From the EFAST2 Web site (http://www.efast.dol.gov) click "Login" on the Welcome screen. Then click "Forgot User ID" and enter the email address that you provided during registration. You will need to provide the answer to your challenge question to view your User ID.

If you have not fully completed the registration process, you will see an option to "Complete Registration" after answering your challenge question.

Q7.   I don't remember my Password. How can I retrieve it?

If you have forgotten your password, or if your password is locked, from the EFAST2 Web site (http://www.efast.dol.gov) click "Login" on the Welcome screen, then click "Forgot Password" on the Login page. To use the "Forgot Password" option, you must enter a valid User ID or registered email address. You will also be prompted to enter the answer to your challenge question. If done successfully, you will be allowed to create a new password.

Q8.   I don't remember my PIN. How can I retrieve it?

After successfully logging in to the EFAST2 Web site, you may view your EFAST2 PIN and other registration information by clicking "User Profile." The User Profile page will display your credentials and provide options to "Change Profile," "Change Password," and "Change PIN."

Q9.   What are the differences among a password, a PIN, and an ETIN?

An EFAST2 password is a 10-16 character password that is created by the registered EFAST2 user. It can be changed using "Forgot Password" on the Login page, or by using "Change Password" on the User Profile page. In conjunction with the assigned User ID, the password is used to log in to the EFAST Web site.

An EFAST2 PIN is a 4-digit number assigned to a registered user. It can be changed by using "Change PIN" on the User Profile page. In conjunction with the assigned User ID, the PIN is used to provide an electronic signature on a Form 5500 or Form 5500-SF.

An EFAST2 ETIN is an Electronic Transmitter Identification Number. The ETIN, along with a PIN, is required for preparers to submit filings or batches of filings on behalf of others using EFAST2-approved third-party software. Filing Authors and Filing Signers normally do not need the ETIN.

Q10. How can I change the address, email address, or user types I entered when I initially registered?

If you need to change your profile information, including the type(s) that are associated with your User ID, first login to the EFAST2 Web site. Click "User Profile," then on the resulting User Profile page click "Change Profile." Don't forget to save your changes when you are finished.

The EFAST2 system does not allow changes to the answer provided to the challenge question (place of birth or date of birth). Also, the EFAST2 User ID itself is a unique, system-generated ID that cannot be changed for an established account.

Q11. I didn't print my registration page that listed my PIN. How can I see my PIN now?

You can view your EFAST2 PIN at any time. After successfully logging in, click "User Profile" to view your PIN at the top of the screen.

Q12. I am not sure if I have already registered. How can I check?

There are multiple ways that you may check to see if you have successfully registered with EFAST2.

If you are not sure that you have successfully completed the registration process, click either "Forgot User ID" or "Forgot Password" on the Login page and enter the email address that you believe you entered during registration.

- If you have registered that email address, you will be prompted to enter the answer to the associated challenge question.

- If you have not registered that email address, you will see an error indicating this email address doesn't match what we have on file.

- If you began registering that email address but have not yet completed the registration process, you will see an option to "Complete Registration" on the screen. Follow the instructions on the remaining screens to complete your registration.

Alternately, you may attempt to complete the registration process by clicking "Register." After you enter the required information, including email address, click "Next." If the email address you have entered is already associated with an EFAST2 account, you will receive the message that the email address you provided is already in use.

Q13. I work for multiple companies but the "Company Name" field will not let me enter both company names, and I can't register for another UserID using the same email address. How can I register for all my companies/plans?

The EFAST2 registration process does not provide a way to add multiple companies to a profile, nor is it necessary for you to do so. Although you provide employment information when registering, the credentials are personal and are not linked to a company or plan. The EFAST2 credentials can be used to identify the registrant for multiple years and on multiple filings. EFAST2 registration allows only one active User ID per valid email account. Each person should need only one active registration.

Q14. What are "User Types" and which should I choose?

Each user type has specific filing tasks associated with it. If the registrant will be performing filing tasks associated with more than one user type, he or she may select multiple user types.

Filing Author: Filing Authors can complete Form 5500/5500-SF and the accompanying schedules, submit the filing, and check filing status. Filing Authors cannot sign filings unless they also have the "Filing Signer" role. If you are using EFAST2-approved third-party software to author your filing rather than IFILE, you do not need to check this box.

Filing Signer: Filing signers are Plan Administrators, Employers/Plan Sponsors, or Direct Filing Entities who electronically sign the Form 5500/5500-SF. This role should also be selected by plan service providers that have written authorization to file on behalf of the plan administrator under the EFAST2 e-signature option. No other filing-related functions may be performed by selecting this user role alone.

Schedule Author: Schedule Authors can complete one or more of the schedules that accompany Form 5500/5500-SF. Schedules created by a Schedule Author are not associated with a filing. For a schedule created by a Schedule Author to be used in a filing, the schedule must be exported. This exported file will then be imported by the Filing Author to the correct filing. Schedule Authors cannot initiate, sign, or submit a filing. If the Filing Author is using EFAST2-approved third-party software to author your filing rather than IFILE, then you do not need to check this box.

Transmitter: Transmitters can transmit Form 5500/5500-SF filings to the EFAST2 system for processing on behalf of others. Transmitters are responsible for the security of all filing information prior to and during its transmission. A Transmitter can be a company, trade, business, or individual.

Third-Party Software Developer: Third-Party Software Developers make Form 5500 filing preparation or transmission software for use in the EFAST2 system. They submit test cases using their software to the Participant Acceptance Testing System (PATS) Team. The PATS Certification Team will then review their submissions and provide feedback, or will approve and certify the software. A Third-Party Software Developer can be a company, trade, business, or individual.

Q15. Do I need to register each year?

No, you should only need to register one time. However, credentials that have never been used for three consecutive calendar years will expire.

Q16. Where can I find more information about EFAST2 credentials?

The EFAST2 Web site contains several Frequently Asked Questions and User Guides. To locate much of this material, including the Instructions for Form 5500, the "EFAST2 Guide for Filers and Service Providers," the "EFAST2 Quick Start Guide," the "EFAST2 IFILE User's Guide," and a link to "EFAST2 Tutorials," please go to **Forms, Instructions, and Publications**.

Appendix G

EFAST REGISTRATION INSTRUCTIONS

The Department of Labor (DOL) requires that all Form 5500 filings be electronically filed and signed. The system they use is known as "EFAST 2". The person that will be signing your Form 5500 must register for filing credentials at the DOL website. Below are instructions for how to obtain filing credentials with the DOL.

Once this process is complete, you can continue to use the UserID and PIN provided by the DOL in future years. If a different person signs the 5500 filing in a future year, that person will have to register with the DOL signing credentials at that time. In addition, more than one person may obtain credentials to sign a 5500 form if more than one person may actually sign the filing. Please note: EFAST will require you to change passwords periodically.

5500 FORM SIGNER CREDENTIAL PROCEDURE

There are several steps to registering on the DOL website. We suggest that you set aside approximately 15 minutes to complete the process. However, please keep in mind that it may take more than 15 minutes as there are several steps in the process. Please also note that the DOL may change the registration process - these are the steps as we currently understand them.

To Begin - Go to **http://www.efast.dol.gov/welcome.html** and click on **Register** found on the left-hand side of the screen.

Step 1 of 7 – **Register - Privacy Statement**. You will be asked to read the statement and acknowledge you did by checking the box to accept the privacy statement. Click the button **Accept Agreement**.

Step 2 of 7 – **Register - Profile Information**. You will be taken to a screen where you will be required to complete information that will serve as your profile (first name, last name, address, email, user type, etc.) and then choose **Next**.

NOTE: In order for a filing to be accepted once signed, you must enter your name as you will enter it upon signing. Ensure that there are no extra spaces surrounding your name (this can generally be avoided by typing out your name and not copying and pasting it).

Filing Signer: Filing signers are Plan Administrators, Employers/Plan Sponsors, or Direct Filing Entities who electronically sign the Form 5500/5500-SF. This role should also be selected by plan service providers that have written authorization to file on behalf of the plan administrator under the EFAST2 e-signature option. No other filing-related functions may be performed by selecting this user type alone.

Step 3 of 7 – **Challenge Information**. You will be asked to select a challenge question and answer. This is required and will be used to obtain your UserID and PIN. Choose Date of Birth of City of Birth, enter the information and then **Next**.

EFAST REGISTRATION INSTRUCTIONS

Step 4 of 7 – Register – Summary Review your profile. When satisfied, choose **Submit**. Check your email. You will receive an email from efast2@efastsys.dol.gov that will instruct you on how to retrieve your PIN and UserID. You will have until a certain date (indicated in the email) to retrieve the UserID and PIN; otherwise, you will have to call 1-866-463-3278 for assistance.

Step 5 of 7 – Register – PIN Agreement. After you click on the link provided in the efast2@efastsys.dol.gov email, you will be directed to a screen where you will answer your challenge question you set up earlier in the process. Read the PIN Agreement. By agreeing to the PIN agreement, you are indicating that you will not share your PIN that has been assigned to you with anyone else. Check the "I have read this agreement" box and then click: **Accept Agreement**.

Step 5a of 7 – Register - Signature Agreement. You will then be asked to agree to a more detailed "Signature Agreement". Check the "I have read this agreement" box and then click **Accept Agreement**.

Step 6 of 7 – Register – Password. Create a password. You will need to create a password that will allow you to log into efast.dol.gov, which completes the process of obtaining the UserID and PIN.

Step 7 of 7 – Register – Confirmation. You should see Successful Account Activation! **Print** the confirmation now! After you have created a password, you will receive your confirmation page that includes your UserID and PIN. We strongly suggest printing this page for your records and keeping your password in a safe place.

Congratulations! You are now registered an able to login in the future.

You can always access your User Profile from the main page by clicking on **User Profile**.

Appendix H

KEY ADMINISTRATIVE DATES
401(k) Plans with Plan Year End of 12/31

January

1/31	Form W-2 to employee
	Form 1099-R to participant
	Form 945 to IRS

February

2/11	Form 1099-R (paper) to IRS
2/28	Form W-2 (paper) to IRS

March

3/15	ADP/ACP Testing Corrections
	Corporate tax return without extension

April

4/11	Required Minimum Distributions (Age 70½)
4/15	Partnership tax return without extension
	Corrective distributions 402(g) excess
	Sole proprietor tax return without extension

May

June

6/30	EACA ADP/ACP Testing corrections

July

7/29	Summary of Material Modifications
7/31	Plan Audit for 5500
	Form 5500 or Form 5558
	Form 8955-SSA or Form 5558
	Form 5330 or Form 5558
	Notice to Terminated Vested Employees

August

September

9/15	Extended deadline Corporate tax returns and contributions
9/30	SAR when 5500 not extended

October

10/1	Safe Harbor Notice
	Automatic Enrollment Notice
10/15	Form 5500 extended deadline
	Form 8955-SSA extended deadline
	Corrective Plan Amendment
	Extended deadline Sole proprietor tax return and contribution deposit for deductibility

November

11/15	Summary Annual Report (SAR)

December

12/1	QDIA Notices
	Last day to distribute Safe Harbor Notices
12/15	Automatic Enrollment Notices
	Begin re-enrollment
	Last day for Required Minimum Distributions (Age 70½)
	Final corrections for failed ADP/ACP tests
	Safe Harbor, QACA or EACA Elections
	Self employed Partner Elections
	Remove Safe Harbor feature
	Discretionary Plan Amendments

Appendix I

NON-CALENDAR YEAR PLANS

When a 401(k) plan does not operate on a calendar year cycle, the complexity of administration, reporting and testing increases dramatically. This translates to additional compliance and administration.

- **CALENDAR YEAR** is a 12 month period running from January 1 to December 31.
  FISCAL YEAR is 12 month period used for tax reporting purposes.
- **NON-CALENDAR YEAR** is a 12 month period that does not run January 1 to December 31.

401(k) Administration becomes more complex and cost increases

One of the major reasons your plan may not operate on a calendar plan year basis is due to your corporate fiscal year. You have a choice to run your plan on a calendar reporting basis or a non-calendar year reporting basis. Most companies whose fiscal year is not calendar, often choose to run the 401(k) on a calendar year basis.

The main reason to operate a plan on a calendar year basis is payroll reporting. It is much simpler to use W-2 reporting, since it is done is on a calendar year basis. This makes internal reporting and administration more efficient and streamlined. Ask any Human Resources or Payroll department involved in coordinating plan year end data. Most often, they will agree non-calendar year plans are complicated. Just because it is a "fiscal" year, doesn't make their job easier related to the 401(k) plan. They must work with the payroll company to provide not only a plan year annual census for their recordkeeping service provider/TPA, but they must also provide a calendar year census.

Implementing non-calendar year plans and their regulations and limitations is very confusing. Below is a simple summary of how they relate to non-calendar year plans.

How Non-calendar plan year affects the 401(k) plan

Elective Deferral – 401(k) deferrals under IRC 402(g) and catch-up contributions are always based on a calendar year (1/01 – 12/31).

415 Limitations – Maximum contribution allocations are applied on a plan year basis, based on the plan year end. If your plan year end is March 2017, the annual limitation is 2016.

Maximum Compensation – Based on the plan year beginning date. For a March 31, 2017 plan year end, the 2016 limitation is used since the first day of the plan year began in the prior year, 2016.

Highly Compensated Employee (HCE) – HCEs are determined based on the "look-back" year (prior year's wages). For a non–calendar year plan, an HCE is based on the look-back limit in effect on the first day of the look-back plan year. Thus, the 2016 limit will apply for determining HCEs for the plan year ending June 30, 2017.

NON-CALENDAR YEAR PLANS

ADP/ACP Testing – Reclassifying a 401(k) contribution to catch-up is based on the plan year end. Hence, for a March 31, 2017 plan year end, the 2017 catch up limit applies.

Contribution Deduction For Corporate Tax Year – The plan year deduction is based on the plan year end. A company with a March 31, 2017 plan year end that deposits their company contribution after the year end but before the end of the calendar year, 2017, would deduct the amount on a 2017 calendar year tax return.

Form 5500 – The Form 5500 will always be the form reflecting the Plan Year beginning date. A company with a March 31, 2017 plan year end will file their Form 5500 using the 2016 Form 5500.

Top Heavy – The test is based on account balances using the first day of the plan year (which is the last day of the preceding year).

Trust Accounting and Plan Audit – If your investment company only reports on standard investment quarters (3/31, 6/30, 9/30 and 12/31), this will cause confusion to plan participants, as their participant statements will not tie out to their year-end summary report. In addition, someone will have to track the investment earnings between two calendar years to arrive at the actual earnings for the non-calendar year 12 month period.

Appendix J

GLOSSARY OF 401(K) TERMS

TERMS	DEFINITIONS
§402(g)	The Internal Revenue Code section that sets a dollar limit on the amount of elective deferrals that a participant may contribute during a calendar year. For 401(k) plans other than SIMPLE 401(k) plans, the limit is $18,000 for 2016. For SIMPLE 401(k) plans, the limit is $12,500 for 2016. The foregoing amounts are increased for participants age 50 and over by permitting additional catch-up contributions described in §414(v).
§414(v)	The Internal Revenue Code section that sets a dollar limit on catch-up contributions that participants may make to a plan during a calendar year. For 401(k) plans other than SIMPLE 401(k) plans, the limit is $6,000 for 2016. For SIMPLE 401(k) plans, the limit is $3,000 for 2016.
§415	The Internal Revenue Code section that sets a limit on a participant's annual additions. The limit is equal to the lesser of 100 percent of compensation and a certain dollar amount. The dollar amount is $53,000 for 2016.
401(k) plan	A defined contribution plan that includes a feature that allows a participant to choose between receiving compensation in cash or deferring it into the plan.
Actual contribution percentage test (ACP Test)	A test to determine whether matching contributions and employee after-tax contributions made on behalf of employees discriminate in favor of highly compensated employees. To perform the test, the average contribution percentage for highly compensated employees for a plan year is compared to the average contribution percentage for nonhighly compensated employees for the same plan year or for the prior plan year, depending on whether the plan is using the current year testing method or the prior year testing method.
Actual deferral percentage test (ADP Test)	A test to determine whether elective deferrals made on behalf of employees discriminate in favor of highly compensated employees. To perform the test, the average deferral percentage for highly compensated employees for a plan year is compared to the average deferral percentage for nonhighly compensated employees for the same plan year or for the prior plan year, depending on whether the plan is using the current year testing method or the prior year testing method.
Advisory letter	A written statement issued by the Internal Revenue Service to a volume submitter practitioner or volume submitter mass practitioner as to the acceptability of the form of a specimen plan and any related trust or custodial account under §401(a).
Affiliated service group	Any group consisting of a service organization ("first organization") and one or more of the following: (1) any service organization (an organization whose principal business is the performance of services) which is a shareholder or partner in the first organization and regularly performs services for the first organization or is regularly associated with the first organization in performing services for third persons; and (2) any other organization if it is performing a significant part of its services for either the first organization or for any service organization described in (1) which are of a type historically performed by employees and 10 percent or more of the interests in such organization are held by persons who are highly compensated employees of the first organization or of the
Annual additions	The sum of all contributions and forfeitures, including elective deferrals and employee aftertax contributions, made to a participant's account(s) for a year. The term does not include investment earnings, loan repayments, rollovers and trustee to trustee transfers.
Audit CAP	A program under the Employee Plans Compliance Resolution System. The program is available to plans under examination, allowing them to correct an error by making correction and paying a sanction.
Automatic contribution arrangement	A feature in a plan whereby a covered employee's compensation is reduced by an amount specified in the plan and contributed to the plan on the employee's behalf unless the employee makes an affirmative election to have a different amount or no amount contributed to the plan. In the case of a 401(k) plan with an automatic contribution arrangement, the amounts withheld from employees' compensation are contributed to the plan as elective deferrals and the percentage of compensation contributed is called the default deferral rate.
Average contribution percentage	The average contribution percentage is the average, expressed as a percentage, of the contribution ratios for a group of employees, either highly compensated employees or nonhighly compensated employees. An employee's contribution ratio is the sum of matching contributions and employee after-tax contributions made for the employee for a plan year divided by the employee's compensation for the year.

GLOSSARY OF 401(K) TERMS

TERMS	DEFINITIONS
Average deferral percentage	The average deferral percentage is the average, expressed as a percentage, of the deferral ratios for a group of employees, either highly compensated employees or nonhighly compensated employees. An employee's deferral ratio is the elective deferrals made for the employee for a plan year divided by the employee's compensation for the year.
Basic matching contribution	A type of safe harbor 401(k) plan contribution. It is a qualified matching contribution equal to the sum of 100% of the participant's elective deferrals that do not exceed 3% of compensation and 50% of the participant's elective deferrals that exceed 3% of compensation but not 5% of compensation.
Cash balance plan	A type of defined benefit plan that describes a participant's accrued benefit as a hypothetical account balance or a single-sum amount.
Catch-up contribution	An elective deferral that exceeds a statutory or plan limit (such as the §402(g) limit) but which is permitted under §414(v) by participants aged 50 or over, provided they have sufficient compensation for the year to make the additional deferral. This additional deferral is limited to
Company	The business that sponsors the 401(k) plan.
Compensation	Pay received by employees of the plan sponsor for personal services. Types of pay includible in compensation are described in the plan document. A plan may have several different definitions of compensation.
Controlled group	A group of trades or businesses (employers) that are related through ownership. A controlled group of employers is either (1) one or more chains of employers connected through ownership with a common parent employer where at least 80% of each employer, other than the common parent, is owned by one or more of the other employers and the common parent owns at least 80% of one or more of the other employers ("parent-subsidiary controlled group"); (2) two or more employers where five or fewer common owners satisfy an 80% common ownership test and a 50% identical ownership test ("brother-sister controlled group"); or (3) three or more employers where each employer is in either a parent-subsidiary controlled group or a brother-sister controlled group and at least one of the employers is the common parent employer in a parent-subsidiary controlled group and is also in a brother-sister controlled group ("combined group").
Corrective distribution	A distribution of funds from the plan to correct a nondiscrimination test or to correct a contribution in excess of a statutory limitation.
Current year testing method	Method of performing the ADP test and ACP test where the highly compensated employees' average deferral percentage and average contribution percentage for a plan year are compared to the nonhighly compensated employees' average deferral percentage and average contribution percentage for the same plan year.
Default	A failure to repay a plan loan in accordance with the provisions specified in the plan document. The document must identify the events that constitute the failure and the parameters for any grace period.
Default deferral rate	In the case of an automatic contribution arrangement in a 401(k) plan, the percentage of compensation, specified in the plan, withheld automatically from a covered participant's compensation (unless the participant elects otherwise) and contributed to the plan as an elective deferral.
Defined benefit plan	A plan under which each participant's benefits are not held in separate accounts, but instead, a formula stated in the plan provides for definitely determinable accrued benefits.
Defined contribution plan	A plan which provides for an individual account for each participant. Benefits are based on the amount contributed to the participant's account, and any income, expenses, gains and losses, and any forfeitures of accounts of other participants which may be allocated to such participant's
Designated Roth contribution	An elective deferral designated as a Roth contribution when contributed to the plan and which is not excludable from gross income.
Determination letter	A written statement issued by the Internal Revenue Service to an employer as to the acceptability of the form of a specific plan and any related trust or custodial account satisfying the tax-qualification requirements under §401(a) and related sections.
Direct foreign investment	An investment made directly in a foreign country. The term includes bank accounts, investment accounts, foreign securities, and other foreign investments. The term includes only direct investments (e.g., foreign investments through a U.S. mutual fund are not included).
Direct rollover	A rollover made from one plan to another plan without being distributed to the participant.
Discretionary match	A matching contribution permitted under the terms of the plan but not required. The plan sponsor can choose whether or not to make a discretionary match on a year-by-year basis. The plan sponsor can also choose the amount of the match that will be made.

GLOSSARY OF 401(K) TERMS

TERMS	DEFINITIONS
Diversification notice	A written notice provided to plan participants that informs them of their right to sell the employer stock in their accounts.
Elective deferral	An amount elected by a participant to be contributed to a plan, thereby deferring the receipt of the cash as income. Elective deferrals can be either pre-tax elective deferrals or designated Roth contributions.
Eligible automatic contribution arrangement (EACA)	A type of automatic contribution arrangement that may be included in a 401(k) plan. Under the feature, a participant may elect to receive a one-time distribution of elective deferrals withheld under the automatic contribution arrangement. The arrangement must satisfy a uniformity requirement and a notice requirement. This arrangement is described in Internal Revenue Code section §414(w).
Employee	A common-law employee of the company that sponsors the 401(k) plan responding to this questionnaire. An employee also includes certain leased employees.
Employee after-tax contribution	A contribution made by an employee that is designated or treated as an after-tax contribution (other than a designated Roth contribution) when made to the plan and that is allocated to an individual account to which attributable earnings and losses are allocated.
Employee Plans Compliance Resolution System (EPCRS)	The program used by the Internal Revenue Service to correct plan errors. The program consists of the voluntary correction program, the self-correction program and audit CAP.
Employee stock ownership plan	A defined contribution plan comprised either of a stock bonus plan or of a combined stock bonus and money purchase pension plan which is designed to invest primarily in employer stock.
Employer	The company that the employees covered by a plan work for. Note that this definition does not include employees of members of the controlled group if not covered by the Plan.
Employer stock	Stock of the company that sponsors the plan, its subsidiary or other member of its controlled group or affiliated service group.
Enhanced matching contribution	A matching contribution under a safe harbor 401(k) plan that provides each participant with a matching contribution that is greater than the basic matching contribution.
EPCRS Revenue Procedure	Revenue Procedure 2008-50, which describes the EPCRS program and provides the rules and procedures for using the program.
Excess benefit plan	A nonqualified deferred compensation arrangement designed solely to provide benefits in excess of the Internal Revenue Code §415 limits.
Fixed match	A matching contribution that is specifically provided for in the plan document and that must be contributed each year unless and until the plan is amended.
Frozen	A plan under which accruals and/or contributions have ceased but assets are still held for participants and beneficiaries.
Hardship distribution	An in-service distribution from the plan which is made because the participant has suffered severe financial difficulty or an extraordinary event as defined by the plan document. In order to make hardship distributions from a plan, the plan must provide for such distributions.
Highly compensated employee	An employee who (1) owned more than 5% of the employer at any time during the year or the preceding year; or (2) in the preceding year, had compensation from the employer in excess of $120,000 (if the preceding year is 2015, $120,000) and, if the employer so chooses, was in the top 20% of employees when ranked by compensation as defined by Internal Revenue Code §415(c)(3).
In-kind distribution	A distribution from the plan that distributes a plan asset instead of cash to the participant. For example, if a participant requests a distribution and receives Company ABC stock instead of cash, this would be an in-kind distribution.
In-service distribution	A distribution that is paid to a participant while he or she is still employed by the plan sponsor.
Installment payments	A series of equal payments from the plan made to a participant or beneficiary until exhaustion of the account balance
Involuntary cash-out	An amount that may automatically be distributed from the plan in a lump sum upon the participant's termination or retirement if it does not exceed a certain dollar amount.
Key employee	An employee who at any time during the plan year is one of the following: (1) an officer of the employer having an annual compensation greater than $170,000 in the case of the 2016 plan year; (2) a 5% owner; or (3) a 1% owner having an annual compensation from the employer in excess of $150,000.

GLOSSARY OF 401(K) TERMS

TERMS	DEFINITIONS
Leased employee	An individual who is not a common-law employee of the business for which he or she performs services and who (1) provides services to the business pursuant to an agreement between the business and a leasing organization; (2) has performed services for the business or any related entity on a substantially full-time basis for a period of at least 1 year; and (3) performs such services under the primary direction or control of the business.
Life annuity	A series of payments, payable at least annually, for the life of the participant, with no benefits payable after the participant's death.
Lump sum	The distribution, in a single payment, of a participant's entire vested accrued benefit under the plan (or what remains of the participant's vested benefit at the time of the single-sum distribution).
Master/prototype plan	A master plan is a plan that is made available by a sponsor for adoption by employers and for which a single funding medium is established for use by all adopting employers. A prototype plan is a plan that is made available by a sponsor for adoption by employers and under which a separate funding medium is established for each adopting employer.
Matching contribution	Employer contributions that are made on account of elective deferrals or employee after-tax contributions.
Minimum contribution	A contribution required to be made to a plan in any year in which it is determined to be top-heavy.
Money purchase pension plan	A money purchase pension plan is a defined contribution plan that is also a type of pension plan. A pension plan must provide for the payment of definitely determinable benefits over a period of years (usually life) after retirement. To satisfy the "definitely determinable benefits" requirement, a money purchase pension plan must provide a fixed contribution formula that is not subject to the employer's discretion and is not geared to the profits of the company.
Multiemployer plan	A plan (1) to which more than one employer is required to contribute, (2) which is maintained pursuant to one or more collective bargaining agreements between one or more employee organizations and more than one employer, and (3) which satisfies other requirements imposed by
Multiple employer plan	A plan sponsored by two or more employers where at least two of the sponsoring employers are not members of the same controlled group.
Nonelective contribution	An employer contribution to a qualified plan that is neither an elective deferral nor a matching contribution (e.g., a discretionary profit-sharing contribution).
Nonhighly compensated employee	An employee who is not a highly compensated employee.
Non-key employee	An employee who is not a key employee.
Nonqualified deferred compensation arrangement	An arrangement, other than a tax qualified plan, under which compensation of an employee is deferred to a later taxable year. The term is not intended to include arrangements that are excepted from Internal Revenue Code section § 409A.
Nonresident alien	An employee who is not a citizen of the United States and has not met either the green card test or the residency test under Internal Revenue Code section §7701(b); and who receives no U.S. source income from the employer.
Nonstandardized master/prototype	A master/prototype plan that is not a standardized plan. See the definition of standardized master/prototype plan.
Opinion letter	A written statement issued by the Internal Revenue Service to a sponsor or master and prototype mass submitter as to the acceptability of the form of a master/prototype plan under §401(a) and, in the case of a master plan, the acceptability of the master trust under §501(a).
Participant	An employee who is eligible to either make contributions to the Plan or to share in employer contributions to the Plan.
Plan trustee	The person who has exclusive authority and discretion to manage and control the assets of the plan; named as such either in the trust document or appointed to the position.
Pre-approved plan	A master, prototype or volume submitter document.
Primary residence loan	Loan used to acquire any dwelling unit which, within a reasonable time, is to be used as the principal residence of the participant.
Prior year testing method	Method of performing the ADP test and ACP test in which the highly compensated employees' average deferral percentage and average contribution percentage for a plan year are compared to the nonhighly compensated employees' average deferral percentage and average contribution percentage for the prior plan year.
Profit-sharing plan	A defined contribution plan that provides a definite predetermined formula for allocating the contributions made to the plan among the participants and for distributing the funds after a fixed number of years, the attainment of a stated age, or upon the prior occurrence of some event such as layoff, illness, disability, retirement, death, or severance from employment.

GLOSSARY OF 401(K) TERMS

TERMS	DEFINITIONS
Qualified automatic contribution arrangement (QACA)	A safe harbor 401(k) plan that is exempt from the ADP test and the ACP test and not subject to the top-heavy rules. It must provide for automatic contributions at a specified level and meet certain employer contribution, notice and uniformity requirements. The default deferral rate must be at least 3% initially, increasing by 1% each plan year until the rate is at least 6%. The default deferral rate cannot exceed 10% and it must be applied uniformly to all covered participants. The employer must make either a nonelective contribution of 3% of compensation to all participants or a matching contribution equal to the sum of 100% of the participant's elective deferrals that do not exceed 1% of compensation and 50% of the participant's elective deferrals that exceed 1% of compensation but not 6% of compensation.
Qualified joint and survivor annuity	An annuity for the life of the participant with a survivor annuity for the life of the spouse that is between 50% and 100% of the amount of the annuity payable for the joint lives of the participant and spouse. If a participant is not married, the annuity is payable for that participant's life.
Qualified matching contributions	Matching contributions that are fully vested when made to the plan and that are subject to the same distribution restrictions as elective deferrals (except for hardship).
Qualified nonelective contributions	Nonelective contributions that are fully vested when made to the plan and that are subject to the same distribution restrictions as elective deferrals (except for hardship).
Recharacterized	A means of correcting a failed ADP test. Excess elective deferrals are treated as distributed from the plan and contributed as employee after-tax contributions subject to the ACP test.
Rollover	The transfer of a qualified plan distribution from one qualified plan or individual retirement arrangement to another qualified plan or individual retirement arrangement.
Safe harbor 401(k)	A type of 401(k) plan that is exempt from the ADP test and the ACP test and not subject to the top-heavy rules. The plan must meet certain notice and employer contribution requirements. The employer must make either a safe harbor nonelective contribution or a qualified matching contribution that is either a basic matching contribution or an enhanced matching contribution. For purposes of this questionnaire, a safe harbor 401(k) plan does not include a QACA or a SIMPLE 401(k) plan.
Safe harbor nonelective contribution	A type of safe harbor 401(k) plan contribution. It is a qualified nonelective contribution equal to 3% of a participant's compensation.
Self-correction program	One of the programs under the Employee Plans Compliance Resolution System that allows plans to correct insignificant errors without approval from the IRS.
SIMPLE 401(k) plan	A type of 401(k) plan that provides for a lower limit on elective deferrals and certain mandatory employer matching or nonelective contributions. A SIMPLE 401(k) plan is deemed to satisfy the ADP and ACP tests.
Standardized master/prototype	A standardized master/prototype plan is a master/prototype plan that provides an adopting employer with limited choices regarding coverage and benefit options. Following the plan's terms, including any options provided under the plan document, will guarantee that the qualification requirements of the Internal Revenue Code are satisfied.
Stock bonus plan	A defined contribution plan established to provide benefits similar to those in a profit-sharing plan, except that benefits under the plan may be distributable in the stock of the employer.
Target benefit plan	A type of money purchase pension plan providing a benefit formula known as the target benefit. The target benefit, used as the basis for determining the employer's annual contribution, is expressed in the same manner as a benefit formula under a defined benefit plan. The employer's contribution for a participant is determined using the target benefit formula and actuarial assumptions stated in the plan.
Term certain annuity	A benefit payout option that provides for a series of payments, payable at least annually, for a specified period of time.
Terminate/Termination	Cessation of the plan and distribution of its assets to participants. A facts and circumstances test is used to ascertain whether a plan has been terminated. For example, a plan is terminated when, in connection with the winding up of the employer's trade or business, the employer begins to discharge his employees. A plan is not terminated merely because an employer sells or otherwise disposes of his trade or business if the acquiring employer continues the plan as a separate and distinct plan of its own, or consolidates or replaces that plan with a comparable plan.
Third-party administrator	A party hired by a plan or its fiduciaries to aid in performing management and/or recordkeeping functions on behalf of the plan.

GLOSSARY OF 401(K) TERMS

TERMS	DEFINITIONS
Unrelated business income	Gross income derived by an organization from: 1) any unrelated trade or business regularly carried on by it, or 2) debt financed property. An unrelated trade or business is any trade or business which in not substantially related to the purpose for which the organization is exempt from tax. Debt financed property is property purchased with borrowed money. If a plan has unrelated business income it may be required to file Form 990-T, Exempt Organization Business Income Tax Return.
Vesting	The degree to which a participant is entitled to a portion of his or her account balance.
Volume submitter plan	A sample plan of a volume submitter practitioner.
Voluntary correction program	A program under the Employee Plans Compliance Resolution System that allows plans to submit an application and fee to the Internal Revenue Service in order to correct a plan error. This program is not available to plans under examination.

Appendix K

401(k) AND PENSION ACRONYMS

ACA	Automatic Contribution Arrangement
ACP	Actual Contribution Percentage
ACR	Actual Contribution Ratio
ACT	Advisory Committee Report on Tax Exempt and Government Entities
ADEA	Age Discrimination in Employment Act
ADP	Actual Deferral Percentage Test
ADR	Actual Deferral Ratio Test
ASG	Affiliated Service Group
ASPPA	American Society of Pension Professionals and Actuaries
AUDIT CAP	IRS Closing Agreement Program
BAPCPA	Bankruptcy Abuse Prevention and Consumer Protection Act of 2005
BPD	Basic Plan Document
CCT	Common Collective Trust
CODA	Cash or Deferred Arrangement
COLA	Cost of Living Adjustment
CRA	Community Renewal Tax Relief Act of 2000
DC	Defined Contribution Plan
DB	Defined Benefit Plan
DB(K)	Defined Benefit and 401(k) combined plan as created by PPA
DECs	Deductible Employee Contributions
DEFRA	Deficit Reduction Act of 1984
DFE	Direct Filing Entity
DFI	Designated Financial Institution
DFVCP	DOL Delinquent Filer Voluntary Compliance Program
DL	Determination Letter
DOL	Department of Labor
EACA	Eligible Automatic Contribution Arrangement
EBAR	Equivalent Benefit Accrual Rate
EBRI	Employee Benefit Research Institute
EBSA	Employee Benefits Security Administration (Known as PWBA until 2/03)
EESA	Emergency Economic Stabilization Act of 2008
EFAST EFAST2	ERISA Filing Acceptance System
EGTRRA	Economic Growth and Tax Relief Reconciliation Act of 2001
EIAA	Eligible Investment Advice Arrangement

401(k) AND PENSION ACRONYMS

EPCRS	Employee Plans Compliance Resolution System
EPCU	Employee Plans Compliance Unit
ERISA	Employee Retirement Income Security Act of 1974
ERPA	Enrolled Retirement Plan Agent
ERTA	Economic Recovery Tax Act of 1981
E-SIGN	Electronic Signatures in Global and National Commerce Act
ESOP	Employee Stock Ownership Plan
FAB	Field Assistance Bulletin
FSO	First Service Organization
FMLA	Family and Medical Leave Act
GATT	Uruguay Round Agreements Act of General Agreement on Tariff & Trade
GOZA	Gulf Opportunity Zone Act of 2005
GUST	GATT, USERRA, SBJPA '96, TRA '97 and IRSRRA
HEART	The Heroes Earnings Assistance and Relief Tax Act of 2008
HERO	Heroes Earned Retirement Opportunities Act of 2006
HAS	Health Savings Accounts
HCEs	Highly Compensated Employees
IRA	Individual Retirement Account as described at Section 408 of the IRC
IRC	Internal Revenue Code
IRSRRA	Internal Revenue Service Restructuring and Reform Act of '98
JCWAA	Job Creation and Worker Assistance Act of 2002
J&S	Joint and Survivor Annuity Rules
KETRA	Katrina Emergency Tax Relief Act of 2005
LLC	Limited Liability Company
LRM	List of Required Modifications
M&P PLAN	A Master Plan or Prototype Plan
NHCEs	Non-Highly Compensated Employees
NIPA	National Institute of Pension Administrators
NRA	Normal Retirement Age
OBRA '87	Omnibus Budget Reconciliation Act of '87
OBRA '93	Omnibus Budget Reconciliation Act of '93
PACMBPRA	Preservation of Access to Care for Medicare Beneficiaries and Pension Relief Act 2010
PBGC	Pension Benefit Guaranty Corporation
PFEA	Pension Funding Equity Act of 2004

401(k) AND PENSION ACRONYMS

PLR	Private Letter Ruling
PPA	Pension Protection Act of 2006
PT	Prohibited Transaction
PTCE	Prohibited Transaction Class Exemption
PWBA	Pension and Welfare Benefits Administration (Renamed EBSA 2/03)
QAB	Quality Assurance Bulletin
QACA	Qualified Automatic Contribution Arrangement
QDIA	Qualified Default Investment Alternative
QDROs	Qualified Domestic Relations Orders
QJSA	Qualified Joint and Survivor Annuity
QMACs	Qualified Matching Contributions
QNECs	Qualified Nonelective Employer Contribution
QOSA	Qualified Optional Survivor Annuity
QPAM	Qualified Professional Asset Manager
QPSA	Qualified Preretirement Survivor Annuity
QRD	Qualified Reservist Distribution
QSLOB	Qualified Separate Line of Business
QTA	Qualified Termination Administrator
RAP	Remedial Amendment Period
RBD	Required Beginning Date
REA	Retirement Equity Act of 1984
REV PROC	Revenue Procedure
REV RUL	Revenue Ruling
RMD	Required Minimum Distribution
ROBS	Rollovers as Business Start-ups
SAR	Summary Annual Report
SARSEP	Salary Reduction Simplified Employee Pension Plan
SBJCA	The Small Business Jobs and Credit Act of 2010
SBJPA	The Small Business Job Protection Act of 1996
SCP	IRS Self-Correction Program
SCRA	Servicemembers Civil Relief Act of 2003
SEC	Securities and Exchange Commission
SEP	Simplified Employee Pension Plan
SEPRA	Single Employer Pension Plans Amendment Act of 1986

401(k) AND PENSION ACRONYMS

SIMPLE	Savings Incentive Match Plan for Employees
SMM	Summary of Material Modifications
SOX	Sarbanes-Oxley Act of 2002
SPD	Summary Plan Description
TAM IRS	Technical Advice Memorandum
TAMRA	Technical and Miscellaneous Revenue Act of 1988
TEFRA	Tax Equity and Fiscal Responsibility Act of 1982
TIPRA '06	Tax Increase Prevention and Reconciliation Act of 2005
TRA '86	The Tax Reform Act of 1986.
TRA '97	The Taxpayer Relief Act of 1997
TREAS REG	Treasury Regulation
TWB	Taxable Wage Base
UBTI	Unrelated Business Taxable Income
UCA	Unemployment Compensation Amendments Act of 1992
USERRA	Uniformed Services Employment and Reemployment Rights Act of 1994
VCP	IRS Voluntary Correction Program
VCR	Voluntary Compliance Resolution
VEBA	Voluntary Employee Benefit Association
VFCP	DOL Voluntary Fiduciary Correction Program
VS	Volume Submitter
WFTRA	Working Families Tax Relief Act of 2004
WRERA	The Worker, Retiree and Employer Recovery Act of 2008

Appendix L

ILLUSTRATION OF THE 401(k) TEAM

Appendix M

The Saver's Tax Credit

Are you saving in a 401(k) or 403(b) Plan?

Did you know you might be eligible for a **tax credit** by making a 401(k) or 403(b) contribution to the plan?

Saving for one's retirement plan is not always a priority. However, there is an added incentive to save for retirement in the form of a non-refundable tax credit known as "the saver's tax credit". A tax credit reduces the amount of tax you owe, unlike a tax deduction that merely reduces the amount of your taxable income. A tax credit is a dollar-for-dollar reduction of taxes owed. It is a non-refundable federal income tax credit available to individuals with an adjusted gross income (AGI) of less than $61,500.

You may be eligible to claim a tax credit of up to $1,000 when you make salary reduction contributions. Your contribution to a 401(k) plan, Simple 401(k), 403(b) plan, governmental 457(b), Simple IRA and SAR-SEP can reduce an individual's AGI, creating Saver's Tax Crdit eligibility. In addition, the credit is available for contributions to traditional IRA or Roth IRA.

The tax credit was created for low-income and moderate-income savers. Again, this credit applies only as a reduction to your income tax liability, not as cash in hand via a refund. If you owe no federal income tax, you are not eligible for a tax credit. In order to qualify for the saver's credit you must be: 18 years of age or older, not a full-time student, and not claimed as a dependent on someone else's return.

If you think you can't afford to save for retirement, think again. Not only could contributing to your retirement plan account at work reduce the federal income tax that comes out of your paycheck, you could also get back up to $1,000 when you file your federal tax return.

2016 Savers Credit Available to Some Taxpayers

Some taxpayers can save for retirement and earn a special tax credit. This credit, referred to as the "saver's credit" can offset the first $2,000 contributed to the taxpayer's IRA, 401(k) and other retirement plans.

The Saver's Credit is like a rebate: Depending on your income and tax filing status, it's worth as much as 50% of every dollar you save for retirement (up to $2,000 for married taxpayers who each save at least $2,000 and file jointly, up to $1,000 for singles).

So, what are you waiting for? Start saving for your future—and earning your credit—today!

There is a catch. The credit is only available to taxpayers which meet certain income criteria. The credit has been available as a permanent fixture since 2006 but the income amounts are indexed each year. Currently, they are:

Married Filing Jointly	Head of Household	Singles and Others	Saver's Credit
AGI up to $37,000	AGI up to $27,750	AGI up to $18,500	50% of your contribution
$37,001 - $40,000	$27,751 - $30,000	$18,501 – 20,000	20% of your contribution
$40,001 - $61,500	$30,001 - $46,125	$20,001 - $30,750	10% of your contribution

To claim the credit, use form 8880 together with your Form 1040. Be sure and read the instructions or consult with your tax advisor.

If you haven't already enrolled in the plan, do it now! Start TODAY.

Talk to your tax advisor to see if you qualify.

ABOUT THE AUTHOR

BARBARA KLEIN, QPA, QKA

Barbara Klein, the founder of 401k Essentials, has 40 years experience in the retirement plan industry. Her breadth of knowledge and experience crosses through many of the 401(k) industry roles. Barbara's diverse background includes working with the government (Social Security Administration), an insurance company, a pension software firm and a third party administration firm. She is a frequent speaker and educator within the pension industry.

In addition to operating 401kEssentials.com business, Barbara owns and operates a third party administration firm in Santa Barbara, California. Accrued Benefit Administrators, Inc. (ABA), operating since 1991, is a full service retirement plan administration firm specializing in qualified retirement and welfare benefit plans. The firm administers all types of retirement plans including - defined contribution and defined benefit plans such as 401(k), 403(b), profit sharing, simple, cash balance and many others.

Barbara is a credentialed pension professional with the designations: Qualified Pension Administrator (QPA) and Qualified 401(k) Administrator (QKA) from the American Society of Pension Professionals & Actuaries.

Professionally, Barbara is a member of the American Society of Pension Professionals & Actuaries, the National Institute of Pension Administrators, the Society of Human Resource Management, National Association of Women Business Owners, Provisors, the Professionals in Human Resources Association, the Santa Barbara Human Resource Association, and the Western Pension & Benefits Conference.

Barbara has won many awards, including most recently the prestigious 2013 Spirit of Entrepreneurship Award and the 2010 Best Small Business - Family Business & Closely Held Company Award.

What People Are Saying About

401(k) ESSENTIALS FOR THE HR PROFESSIONAL

"Long after the plan is sold/installed, our human resource professionals are responsible for the various day to day complexities involved in running a 401(k). However, I've noticed that many HR professionals lack the required training and resources needed to handle what could potentially create liability to the company! Barbara has hit the mark. Assistance is now available from one of the most experienced practitioners in the industry!"

— **Roger Rocha, Regional VP,
VOYA FINANCIAL**

"HR professionals, take heart! Finally, there's a very simple and easy book and reference tool that explains 401(k) plans for the plan sponsor. Written in plain English (in case you don't speak fluent 'pensionese') the book explains the major (and minor) points of 401(k) plans. Each chapter has a brief questionnaire that helps you relate the materials to your company's plan. This book also outlines the roles and responsibilities you have in running the 401(k) plan, a boon to most HR professionals. Easy to read and understand, the book is thorough, well laid out and sufficiently detailed to give you confidence that you understand and can handle your 401(k) plan.

"We've been waiting for this book for 30 years! Thank you, Barbara Klein. All your years administering 401(k) plans pays off handsomely in this great tool for HR professionals charged with handling the company 401(k) plan. Wish I had thought of it first!"

— **Nancy Michael, Principal,
COMMUNICATIONS INK, Glendale, CA**

"This book will allow the user to gain a much needed sense of comfort, which is so desperately being sought after in today's climate. Anything you can do to relieve the administrative burden by arming them with what they need is a valuable service."

— **Tristan Smith, TPA Regional
Marketing Director – Pacific
JOHN HANCOCK FINANCIAL
SERVICES**

"Congratulations on this new venture. It looks like it can't lose. Good material for the HR professional is essential in this area. You are filling a void that is essential to proper delivery of retirement benefits."

— **Sal L. Tripodi, J.D., LL.M.,
TRI PENSION SERVICE and author of
*The ERISA Outline Book***

"***401(k) ESSENTIALS*** is a terrific handy reference guide. It is a must have for all 401(k) plan sponsors; quick, simple explanations to complex material. This is a great resource, well written, and comprehensive. I highly recommend it."

— **Eric P. Chappell, Attorney at Law,**
CHAPPELL & CHAPPELL

"I've had the privilege of working with Barbara in the retirement plan industry for over 25 years and know first-hand of her professional expertise and retirement plan industry knowledge. Barbara's extensive experience in qualified plan regulations and administration, as well as her desire to help make her clients' job easier, uniquely equip her with the skills and expertise to assist plan sponsors with just the right amount of information at the right time. She's the consummate teacher, having the wonderful ability to convey the essentials of what is important to her clients and associates in a very clear and concise manner!"

— **Mary Turley, Sales Consultant,**
ASC SOFTWARE (Actuarial Software Corporation)

"I can't believe no one thought of this before. Barbara Klein and her team have hit the mark with ***401(k) ESSENTIALS***. If you are responsible for overseeing a 401(k) plan, you must check out the book and the website. Sign up now."

—**Debbie Allen, International Business Speaker & Bestselling Author**

"I met Barbara when I joined the Goleta Noontime Rotary Club. Her commitment to making our Club the best in our district was evident from the start. She takes on projects even when her plate is already full. It doesn't matter if the tasks are mundane. She puts the same energy and effort into making them perfect. It exemplifies her integrity. She gives of her time to friends and family with abandon. Now she has written a book sharing her knowledge with her contemporaries. I am more than impressed. Read what she has to offer. You will not be disappointed."

— **Barbara Tzur, President,**
BRYLEN TECHNOLOGIES

"Barbara is among the most qualified and professional retirement plan administrators I've known. I had the pleasure of working closely with Barbara and have first-hand knowledge of her knowledge, integrity and attention to detail. I highly recommend Barbara and her firm to fulfill the retirement plan administrative needs of any organization."

— **Larry DuBois, (Retired) Founder and President of PENTABS**

Customer Reviews

5.0 out of 5 stars

⭐⭐⭐⭐⭐

Top Customer Reviews

⭐⭐⭐⭐⭐ **Great Introductory Source**

By Canthro on July 16, 2015

I was pleased with the scope of the book. It is a perfect amount of introductory information for a new administrator.

⭐⭐⭐⭐⭐ **Incredibly thorough and easy to read. I now have a resource to find...**

By Philip McFadden on October 28, 2015

I never knew what I didn't know until I read this book. Incredibly thorough and easy read. I now have a resource to find answers to so many questions. This book is full of examples and easy to understand explanations. I found all of the deadlines super useful. Just having this knowledge has helped me tremendously in working with employees as well as with my outside partners. 401(k) operations are complex and time consuming, and this book has made the entire process easier to understand and much more efficient.

⭐⭐⭐⭐⭐ **This book is great for the HR Professional or brand new Retirement Plan...**

By Mary on October 6, 2015

This book is great for the HR Professional or brand new Retirement Plan Administrator. It is not good for a seasoned Retirement Plan Administrators. It does not show you how to perform any calculations such as ADP, Top Heavy, Annual Additions etc. No formulas are given. But I highly recommend it for HR Professionals.

SUBSCRIBE TODAY
401kEssentials.com

401kEssentials.com is designed to assist the human resource professional, the benefits specialist and the 401(k) plan sponsor's internal point of contact, tasked with overseeing the company's 401(k) plan. It will fast become your practical go-to resource for the internal administration of your 401(k) plan. Check it out today!

| Plan Sponsor | HR | Fiduciary | Payroll | Financial Advisor | TPA |

Training. Tools. Peace of Mind.
Designed for HR, Payroll, Plan Fiduciaries, Plan Sponsors, Advisors.

Do you need a quick lesson on a retirement plan feature, some 401(k) industry statistics for a board meeting or a reminder of an upcoming deadline? 401kEssentials.com is here to support you! Whether you prefer to read, watch a video or listen to some tips, 401kEssentials.com provides all these tools in a variety of easy-to-use multi-media formats, and so much more.

Look   Listen   Learn

Born from the desire to share their knowledge, 401kEssentials.com was developed by pension professionals with over 40 years of experience in the pension industry. This service is designed to work in tandem with your 401(k) team members - TPA, CPA, attorney, recordkeeper, investment advisors and investment company. It also serves to educate plan fiduciaries on basic 401(k) concepts, terminology and other aspects of plan operation.

SIGN UP TODAY!

401kEssentials.com

NOTES

NOTES

NOTES

NOTES

NOTES

SHOP THE BOOKSTORE
CHECK OUT ALL THE BOOKS

https://401kEssentials.com/category/books

Our Essentials book series are written to educate and guide you in understanding the operation and administration of qualified retirement plans. Each book is thorough, easy to read, and contains practical explanations of how things work.

- ☑ **401(k) ESSENTIALS FOR THE HR PROFESSIONAL**
- ☑ **401(k) ESSENTIALS FOR THE PAYROLL PROFESSIONAL**
- ☑ **403(b) ESSENTIALS FOR THE ERISA PLAN**
- ☑ **7 MUST HAVES BEFORE AN IRS 401(k) AUDIT**

401(k) Essentials: While dedicated to the HR Professional, it is written for everyone who oversees or is tasked with the management of a 401(k) plan at the plan sponsor's office. Although you hire outside professionals to administer the 401(k) plan, the employer and plan sponsor must understand their plan. This book covers the operational requirements of a 401(k) plan and provides the detail needed to become familiar with the terminology, operations, deadlines, processes, files and much more. Every plan sponsor and fiduciary should have this book in their library.

401(k) Payroll Essentials: This book is a comprehensive guide with practical tools and training to manage and prevent complex 401(k) administration mistakes that can lead to IRS audits. This book is a one-volume desk reference written in plain English. It contains easy to understand and ready to deploy practical guidance regarding the internal payroll administration of a company's 401(k) plan.

403(b) Essentials: 403(b) plans that have accounts containing employer contributions including matching contributions are subject to the rules of ERISA. This book is for the non-profit, educational, hospitals or church organizations that offer their employees a 403(b) plan which is subject to ERISA. It is written for anyone who oversees or is tasked with the management of the 403(b) plan. Written in a practical, clear and understandable manner, this book simplifies the complexities of 403(b) compliance requirements. *To be released Summer 2016.*

7 Must Haves: The potential for an audit of your 401(k) plan is something that every company faces. This booklet provides the information needed to prepare for this inevitable event. By following these tips ahead of time, your records will be up-to-date, data will be easily accessible, and you minimize the monetary cost and the time needed to prepare for an audit.

Made in the USA
Middletown, DE
23 January 2017